A Parent's Guide to Online Safety

Simple Steps to Protect Your Kids From Online Predators, Cyberbullies, Social Media and Gaming Scams

Alex East

Contents

Introduction

Our children are growing up in a world that is very different from the one we have known. This is the "digital age." Where we once played in physical playgrounds with swings and slides, our kids frequent virtual playgrounds where a few simple clicks can open up a world of possibilities and potential dangers.

A seemingly innocent game download can lead to personal information being shared. A chat in a multiplayer game can turn into something far more serious. Fake profiles, scams that look like real messages, apps that track locations without asking, these are becoming more common than ever.

As a cybersecurity professional with over 15 years of experience, I've worked alongside leading cybersecurity firms, large corporations, and government agencies. I've witnessed the evolving tactics of online scammers and predators who relentlessly target the youth and the elderly. I've seen firsthand how clever and persistent scammers and predators can be. Having spent my career dissecting cyber threats, I've seen the damage that can be inflicted on unsuspecting individuals who may not yet have the knowledge or experience to recognize digital dangers and the toll they take on families.

But beyond my professional background, I am also a parent. Like you, I have worried about my children's safety online. I have asked myself the same questions countless other parents have:

Are my kids safe when they're playing their favorite games?

What information are they sharing?

Who are they chatting with?

Why are they on their phones all the time?

These are real-life issues that we face daily as parents.

Keeping kids safe in the age of the internet isn't just about downloading security software, blocking websites, or setting up a password for online accounts. The reality is, even with every tool in place, kids can still run into things we wish they hadn't. What matters just as much is teaching them how to be safe is helping them understand the risks, the red flags, and the choices they make. That's what builds long-term protection.

In my previous book, , I focused on helping older adults protect themselves from digital threats and equipping them with the knowledge and tools to do so. However, as I spent more time researching how cybercriminals operate and how they pick their targets, I realized that children, sometimes as young as 3, face a veritable minefield of threats as well. These cyber threats have been specifically designed to target and exploit children's weaknesses, making things look fun and harmless when they are anything but. It could be tricking them into sharing personal information through fake gaming rewards, luring them into chatting with people who seem friendly, or signing up for things without realizing what they're giving away. This is exactly why I wrote this book: to help you **understand, anticipate, and combat** the daily risks your kids face online. My experience allows me to break down complex cybersecurity measures into actionable steps that any parent can follow. With this knowledge, you can be your kid's first line of defense, both online and offline.

The alarming reality of online threats

The statistics surrounding online threats to children are disturbing. According to the FBI, approximately 500,000 online predators are active daily, each seeking to exploit vulnerable children. A study by the National Center for Missing and Exploited Children found that online predators targeted 59% of children who were 15 years old or younger, with many predators using popular social media and gaming apps to reach their victims.

Even more concerning is the rise of "sextortion" cases, where predators deceive minors into sharing explicit content and then use it for blackmail. In 2023 alone, Homeland Security Investigations reported over 26,000 cases. That's nearly triple the number from the year before, showing just how fast this kind of abuse is growing.

These figures prove that our children are at significant risk, and it's crucial that we, as parents and guardians, equip ourselves with the knowledge and tools to protect them. While it's tempting to respond to growing cyber threats by tightening control over your kid's use of devices or "just take the phone away" altogether, you need to remember that technology is now a part of our lives. It is how kids learn, grow, and connect. It's how they explore ideas, keep up with their peers, and find their voice in a world that increasingly runs on screens. The answer cannot be to cut them off from that world. It's to help them move through it wisely.

All this data and the responsibility of protecting your child from the advanced, vicious, and methodical cybercrimes happening out there can be unavoidably overwhelming, especially when your kid seems light-years more digitally tech-savvy than you are. But here's the good news: You don't need to be a tech expert to keep your family safe online. That's where this book comes in.

A Parent's Guide to Online Safety is specifically designed for parents of children and teens aged 8 to 18. Its purpose: to bridge the digital literacy gap and empower you with practical strategies to protect your kids from the myriad of online threats, from cyberbullying and social media scams to vicious online predators.

Some of the topics we will cover in this book include:

Social media dangers: How predators and scammers use fake personas to worm their way into your children's lives and exploit them.

Online gaming risks: How in-game chatrooms and purchases expose kids to hackers, scammers, and inappropriate content.

Cyberbullying: How online harassment works. How to guide your child to handle it effectively.

Sextortion and exploitation: How to identify the warning signs of manipulation. What to do next if your child is targeted.

Data privacy and security: How to manage your digital footprints. How to secure your home network, strengthen passwords, and protect you and your child's personal information.

In this book, I'm not just going to provide a list of dangers; I'll also give you practical steps to develop healthy online habits, including:

Creating a safe digital environment: Learn how to set up parental controls, filter content, and monitor online activity without invading your child's privacy.

Having the difficult conversations: How to talk to your kids about sexting, pornography, and illegal downloads.

Managing screen time: Find out how to set realistic screen-time limits that encourage a balanced relationship with technology.

Preventing and responding to cyber incidents: Develop a family action plan for dealing with cyber threats, from data breaches to online harassment.

This book contains true stories I have collected on the way (with names and details changed to protect anonymity), provided by the family and friends of those who had to experience an unfortunate cyber incident first-hand. These case studies will help you recognize red flags and serve as cautionary tales.

With *A Parent's Guide to Online Safety*, you'll have a comprehensive understanding of the digital world your kid navigates daily. By the time you finish this book, you'll be well on your way to enjoying the peace of mind that comes with knowing you have the skills to protect them.

Alex East

Author and Cybersecurity expert

CHAPTER 1

Why Children Are Targets

And who is targeting them

If you have ever watched an Animal Planet special, you know that predators don't chase the strongest. They always go after the weakest in the herd. In the online world, children are among the most vulnerable users due to their natural curiosity, naïveté, and limited understanding of online risks. Cybercriminals, predators, and scammers exploit these traits for financial, emotional, or other illicit gains. The first step in keeping kids safe is understanding why they're such prime targets and who is targeting them.

Heavy online presence coupled with limited awareness

Remember when our parents told us not to accept candy from strangers? These days, "candy" comes in many forms online. Kids are naturally curious, open, and eager to connect. Their curiosity and openness are part of what makes childhood special. But on the internet, those same traits can put them at risk.

Kids don't yet have the instincts or experience to spot red flags — the kinds we've learned to watch for. A pop-up offering a reward in their favorite online game seems harmless to them. To us, it screams danger. But for a child, it can feel like just another part of being online. Also, children don't have the expertise and technical knowledge to recognize scams, phishing attempts, or manipulative online behaviors. Unlike adults, they may not be skeptical of offers that seem too good to be true or messages from strangers. Their trust in others makes them particularly vulnerable to deceptive tactics used by online predators.

Almost all children now have smartphones, tablets, gaming consoles, or social media accounts, sometimes all four. They spend more time online than playing outdoors. This increased *digital footprint* makes them more accessible to bad actors. Social media platforms, online games, and messaging apps, most of which have not been designed with child safety as their priority, provide multiple entry points for cybercriminals and predators to initiate contact. More often than not, children are led to click on malicious links, download harmful software, or engage with suspicious individuals without realizing the risks involved.

Children's natural inclination to explore new content and connect with peers means they may join public forums, accept "friend requests" from strangers, or participate in online communities where monitoring is limited or absolutely nonexistent.

An intense desire for social acceptance

Peer approval matters a lot to kids especially in their early teens or when they are just about to enter that stage. Kids care a lot about what their friends think — every like and share on their social media profile means something to them. That's just how it is when you're growing up. And social media plays right into that. It's where they talk to friends, share their lives, and see how others are living theirs. It's also where they measure themselves, by likes, comments, and who's paying attention.

The thing is, that need to be *seen* and *liked* makes them more open to pressure. And there are people online who know exactly how to take advantage of that. Scammers and predators don't come off creepy at first. They act friendly. They give compliments. They know what kids want to hear. Whether through flattery, false promises, or *social engineering* tactics, they exploit children's desire for validation and acceptance.

Sometimes they pretend to be someone the same age. Other times they act like a cool adult who "gets it." They might say things like "you seem really mature" or "you're different from other kids." Stuff that makes a kid feel important. Then they start asking for things, maybe a photo, or personal piece of information, or to keep chatting in private.

Even if children do not own financial assets, they can be a gateway to their parents' sensitive information. Hackers target children to gain access to family financial details or personal data. Children are more likely to share their home address, phone number, or family details without recognizing the risks. Cybercriminals also use children's compromised accounts as stepping stones to infiltrate household networks and gain unauthorized access to financial resources. Teaching children about safeguarding personal information is critical in preventing identity theft and cyber fraud.

Who is Targeting Children?

Different types of malicious individuals target children for various reasons. Understanding their motivations and methods can help us guard against these threats.

Online Predators

Online predators seek to manipulate, exploit, or control children for illegal or abusive purposes. They aim to form emotional connections that enable them to groom their victims. They pressure minors into providing personal information, explicit images, or even meeting in person.

Methods Used: Predators use grooming techniques and friendly conversations to build trust (*catfishing*). They often pose as peers or influential figures to gain access to victims. Many predators operate within gaming platforms, social media, and messaging apps, where children spend significant time.

Once a child trusts them, they escalate their tactics to request photos, demand secrecy, or introduce explicit conversations. Some use blackmail, known as *sextortion* (more on this later), to coerce children into compliance.

Scammers

Scammers target children for financial gain, identity theft, and data harvesting. Some want quick cash. Others are after personal info they can sell or use to open fake accounts. Kids are easy targets because they don't always understand how money works online or what's risky to share.

Methods Used: Common scams targeting children include phishing emails, fake giveaways, and fraudulent online purchases. Many scammers use gaming platforms to manipulate children into purchasing virtual goods or providing financial details.

Scammers pretend to be people kids trust. They'll pose as influencers, game support agents, even celebrities. If someone sounds official, like a customer support rep or a YouTuber they follow, kids are more likely to trust them. And when a kid believes it's someone legit, they might share their login info without thinking twice.

What's worse than financial loss is identity theft. Some scammers grab personal details, like a child's name, birthdate, or even their social security number, and use it to open fake credit accounts. And because no one's checking a kid's credit, it can go unnoticed for years.

Cyberbullies

Cyberbullies target children to cause emotional distress, gain social dominance, or seek revenge. They use digital platforms to harass, embarrass, or isolate victims.

Methods Used: Cyberbullying can take many forms, including public humiliation and *doxxing* (publishing private information online). Sometimes it's nonstop messages meant to wear a kid down. Sometimes, it's rumors being spread to hurt their reputation. It could be someone sharing private photos or personal details without permission. In some cases, bullies even pretend to be the person they're targeting, creating fake accounts to embarrass or manipulate their victim.

Online platforms provide a space where bullies can remain anonymous, which makes it difficult for victims to escape their harassment. The bullying can follow them into their room, into their phone, into the middle of dinner.

It's easy for adults to underestimate how painful cyberbullying can be. To a young person, their online world *is* their world. When that space turns toxic, the emotional weight is heavy. Some kids withdraw. Some start to believe the awful things said about them. The impact can show up as anxiety, depression, sleep problems, or worse. In extreme cases, kids unfortunately harm themselves because they are unable to see a way out of intense cyberbullying.

Data Harvesters

Data harvesters aren't always obvious criminals. They are after a child's clean credit history, email credentials, school logins, or even location data. A child's data is more valuable than an adult's on the dark web. Some identity thieves go further by stealing credentials through phishing attacks and gaining unauthorized access to email accounts and online profiles. Once data is harvested, it is used for identity fraud or sold to marketers or cybercriminals.

Methods Used: Data harvesting has many forms. Sometimes it's a shady app that asks for too many permissions. Sometimes it's a fake survey that looks like a fun quiz. Even free games can quietly track what a child is doing, where they are, how often they play, and what kind of content they're drawn to. All that information can be packaged up and sold to advertisers, marketers, or, in some cases, cybercriminals.

A History of Online Attacks on Minors

Understanding the past is the best predictor of the future. Knowing where we have come from is crucial to understanding the dangers and how they evolve.

Early social media exploitation (2000s)

With the advent of platforms like MySpace, Friends Reunited, and early iterations of Facebook, social media became a new frontier for predators seeking to exploit children.

In 2006, a high-profile case involved a 13-year-old girl named Megan Meier, who was cyberbullied through a fake MySpace account created by an adult in her neighborhood. Tragically, the harassment led Megan to commit suicide. The event made national headlines and highlighted how online interactions allow adults to masquerade as peers.

The Webcam Blackmail epidemic (2010s)

The proliferation of video communication tools, such as Skype and Facetime, introduced new risks, notably the rise of sextortion.

In 2012, Canadian teenager Amanda Todd became a victim after an online predator convinced her to expose herself on a webcam. The individual captured images and used them to blackmail her for several years, leading to relentless cyberbullying and her subsequent suicide. Amanda's story highlighted the severe emotional toll of online exploitation and spurred global discussions on the need for better protective measures for children online.

Gaming exploitation (2015-Present)

Online gaming platforms have become fertile grounds for predators due to their popularity among children.

In 2017, reports emerged of predators using games like Fortnite and Minecraft to approach children. These individuals pose as fellow gamers, gradually building trust before moving conversations to private channels or persuading children to share personal information. Law enforcement agencies have conducted numerous sting operations to apprehend such predators, underscoring the need for parental awareness and platform-level safeguards.

The Blue Whale Challenge

Around 2016, reports surfaced about the Blue Whale Challenge, a supposed social media game that allegedly encouraged participants to engage in self-harm over 50 days.

In July 2017, *CNN* reported on the death of a teenager whose family believed the Blue Whale Challenge influenced her suicide. The article highlighted the family's search for answers and the potential role of the online game in their daughter's death.

While many experts now believe the phenomenon was largely a hoax amplified by sensationalist media, the panic it induced was real. Some vulnerable teens reportedly engaged in self-harming behaviors they believed were linked to the challenge. This incident underscores the potential for misinformation to spread online and the importance of educating children about discerning credible information and the dangers of participating in harmful online trends.

"Elsagate" controversy

In 2017, the Elsagate involved YouTube videos that appeared to be child-friendly but contained disturbing content. These videos featured popular children's characters in violent or sexual scenarios, cleverly bypassing YouTube's content filters and reaching young audiences. The widespread outrage led to YouTube implementing stricter content guidelines and moderation practices. This incident highlights the necessity for parents to monitor their children's online viewing habits and for platforms to enforce strict and effective content filtering.

TikTok and Instagram Era (2020s)

In 2023, the "Benadryl Challenge" on TikTok sparked several incidents where children were encouraged to consume excessive amounts of the medication to induce hallucinations. This dangerous trend led to hospitalizations and at least one reported death.

In parallel, predators actively use these platforms to reach minors, often blending into the environment with alarming ease. On TikTok, they engage through *duets*, *stitches*, and *comment* sections. On Instagram and Snapchat, predators exploit *story replies*, *Snap streaks*, or *mutual follows* to build rapport. These interactions start casually by reacting to a post, sharing a meme, or commenting on a shared interest and slowly shift toward more private, personal, and often harmful conversations.

Chapter 2

Top 10 Cyberattacks Aimed at Minors

And what to look out for

This chapter breaks down the kinds of attacks and tactics that specifically target children and teens online. Some are obvious; others are surprisingly subtle.

Understanding how these attacks work—and *why* they work—is essential. Predators and scammers rely on certain patterns of behavior, both in how they approach kids and how kids typically respond. The more you know about the psychology behind these attacks, the easier it becomes to spot them from a distance.

When you understand the methods, you're in a better position to explain them to your child in a way that actually sticks. That knowledge and awareness can mean all the difference as your child grows and starts navigating the internet more independently.

Grooming

Grooming is a manipulative process used by predators to gain a child's trust for eventual exploitation. It is a calculated and deliberate strategy. It is designed to break down a child's natural barriers, making them more susceptible to manipulation.

Grooming unfolds over an extended period. Predators "groom" their victims to create a sense of secrecy, dependency, and control, ultimately making the child feel complicit or too afraid to seek help.

How does grooming work?

Kids and teens, especially, are wired for connection. They're figuring out who they are, looking for approval, and often craving attention from someone, something very human. Grooming works because it taps into our basic need to be seen and valued.

The process typically follows a series of steps, though each case may vary. These steps often include:

Targeting the child: Predators seek out children who appear vulnerable, lonely, or in need of attention. They often target victims through social media, gaming platforms, chat rooms, and even child-friendly forums.

Gaining trust: Groomers present themselves as caring and understanding figures, positioning themselves as mentors, friends, or romantic partners. Predators often use phrases like *"I feel like I can talk to you about anything"* to build emotional trust. It might be a steady stream of compliments, inside jokes, late-night chats, or moments that feel emotionally deep. To a young person, this is a friend who "just gets them." But the goal here is not friendship, it's control.

A sense of exclusivity: Groomers often make a child feel like they're chosen and different from the rest. They deliberately build emotional dependency with things like *"Let's keep this between us; it's just our thing."* They create a private bubble where the child starts to trust the predator more than anyone else.

Isolation: Once that bond is in place, the next step is distancing the child from people who might raise a red flag. This is done by undermining the child's trust in authority figures or discouraging them from discussing their online interactions with parents. The child is manipulated to increasingly question their parents' intentions and discouraged from talking to friends. This is done with a seemingly well-meaning *"They'd just ruin what we have."* Over time, the child starts pulling away from family, becoming more withdrawn or defensive about who they're talking to. The predator establishes that they are the one voice the child listens to, while everyone and everything else fades into the background.

Desensitizing: Predators gradually introduce sexual topics disguised as jokes or innocent discussions. The predator slowly works to normalize things that shouldn't be normal, private chats, inappropriate questions, sharing personal photos. They send inappropriate images or request the child to do so, making the child feel increasingly comfortable with the exploitation.

Control and manipulation: The predator achieves a strong grip on the child's emotions. They know which buttons to press, be it guilt, fear, or shame, to keep the child quiet. Then the threat becomes obvious. It becomes less about trust and more about control, and the child feels trapped and too scared or ashamed to reach out for help. The predator starts openly and actively escalating their demands.

True story: A thwarted grooming attempt

While researching this book, a mother from San Francisco contacted me to share her story:

Two years ago, Lisa noticed something unusual about her 13-year-old daughter Emily's online habits. Emily had started spending long hours on her phone, and often received messages from someone she called "a friend from a game." When Lisa asked about this "friend," Emily became defensive.

Something didn't feel right, so she asked to see Emily's phone. After a lot of defensive arguments from Emily, Lisa finally managed to convince her daughter that she just wanted to understand what was going on. Then, on patiently examining Emily's texts, Lisa found that her daughter had been messaging a boy called Kayden. However, the boy's stories were inconsistent. He was reluctant to use video calls and frequently changed personal details. Lisa then conducted a reverse image search (where you take an image and use it to search for other, similar images) on the profile pictures he had sent Emily and found that they were stock images taken from the internet.

"Kayden" had first contacted Emily through a chat feature in an online multiplayer game. They had bonded over shared gaming interests and gradually moved their conversation to private messaging apps. Over time, he showered Emily with compliments and small digital gifts, such as in-game currency and exclusive items. He gained her trust by acting like a supportive friend, listening to her problems and making her feel special.

Understanding the seriousness of the situation, Lisa immediately took action. She saved all the messages and contacted law enforcement. Authorities were able to track the predator, who had been grooming multiple children like Emily. Because of Lisa's vigilance, Emily was saved from a dangerous situation, and the predator was arrested.

Phishing and SMiShing

Phishing and SMiShing are two of the most prevalent cyber threats facing adults and children today. Cybercriminals send a fabricated email (phishing) or a text message (SMiShing) in an attempt to trick individuals into revealing sensitive information, such as passwords, personal details, or financial data, often by impersonating trusted entities. Identity theft occurs when someone's personal information is stolen and misused, frequently leading to financial loss, reputational damage, or unauthorized access to private accounts.

How does phishing work?

Phishing and its text-based cousin, SMShing, commonly involve harmful links or fake support numbers. While adults fall for these scams too, kids and teens can be especially vulnerable. They're still learning what *normal* online communication looks like, and they may not question the authenticity of something that seems urgent or exciting.

Scammers use a few common tactics in phishing:

Impersonation scams: These involve attackers pretending to be from legitimate institutions, such as banks, schools, or popular social media platforms. The attackers urge the victim to act immediately, such as verifying an account or updating payment details.

Emotional manipulation: Scammers are good at pushing emotional buttons. They create fear, urgency, or pressure (*"Act fast or lose your gaming account!"*). The goal is to get the child to act before they think.

Malicious links and attachments: Clicking on fraudulent links or downloading attachments can install malware on a device, giving hackers access to sensitive data.

Credential harvesting: Fake login pages are designed to look like legitimate websites. When users enter their credentials, the hacker captures the information for misuse.

True story: Claim your prize!

Phishing scams targeting young gamers are becoming increasingly common, mainly through platforms like Discord, Steam, and gaming forums. These scams often impersonate official game companies or trusted community members to steal login credentials and financial information.

One real-world example involved Jake, a 14-year-old online gamer, who was targeted through a Discord phishing scam. One evening, Jake received a DM (Direct Message) on Discord from a user with the name *GameRewardsBot#2413*. The message read:

"Congratulations! You've been selected for an exclusive in-game giveaway! You've been awarded 5,000 in-game coins and a legendary skin as a dedicated player. Claim it now before it expires in 2 hours! [Claim Here]."

Jake excitedly clicked the provided link. It directed him to a website that perfectly mimicked the official game login page. He entered his username and password. Although what followed wasn't visible on Jake's screen, the moment he submitted his credentials, they were sent directly to the scammer. Within minutes:

The hacker logged into his account, changed the password, and enabled two-factor authentication (2FA) to their email.

Jake was locked out of his account.

Since the gaming platform was linked to his mother's credit card, the scammer made over $300 in fraudulent in-game purchases before the card was frozen.

When Jake's mother contacted customer support, it was too late. The game company refunded some unauthorized purchases, but their policy did not allow account recovery if security measures were bypassed. Jake permanently lost access to his game progress, purchased items, and personal data. This also meant that Jake's account could have been used to contact his friends and other gamers, posing as him.

Catfishing

Catfishing is when someone creates a fake online identity to trick others. Most people think of it in the context of online dating, but it can just as easily affect kids and teens, and the risks are serious. Predators, cyberbullies, and scammers use catfishing to gain trust, extract personal information, and exploit their victims emotionally or financially.

How catfishing works?

Creating a fake identity: The catfisher constructs a convincing false persona using stolen photos and fabricated details. Their profile appears trustworthy and relatable to children. Advanced catfishers even use AI-generated voices and altered videos to make their fake identities even more convincing.

Building trust: Once contact is made, they start putting in time. They chat often, pretend to share common interests, and say all the right things. Over time, this creates a sense of emotional closeness and dependence. They carefully use excuses to avoid video calls or in-person meetings, maintaining their false identity.

Extracting personal information: Then comes the request for personal details, sometimes subtly sometimes directly. It could be an address, the name of school, or even financial information. The catfisher takes great care to make this feel like part of the relationship.

Exploit: The catfisher starts asking for money, gifts, or explicit photos or videos. Because the child believes there's a real connection, they go along with it, not realizing they're being used.

True story: Catfisher gets caught

Sixteen-year-old John from Seattle, Washington, thought he had made a true friend online. Like many teenagers, John spent his free time on TikTok, engaging with people who shared his interests. One day, he connected with a user who claimed to be a 15-year-old girl from Ohio. Over several months, their online friendship deepened. They chatted daily, shared personal details, and built what John believed was his first love.

One day, suddenly the girl said she had racked up a massive phone bill and was terrified her parents would kick her out if they found out. She told him that she had no one else to turn to. She said that unless she could come up with the money, she would no longer be able to contact him. John, eager to help the girl he loved and prove his loyalty, sent her $250.

In the days that followed, the requests came thick and fast; she wanted to watch a Netflix show with him, but her parents wouldn't let her subscribe, and many more similar predicaments that required a payment she didn't have. John sent her payments using gift cards and Cash App transfers each time. By the time the requests became almost daily, he had drained over $1,500 from his savings account.

When the demands for money continued, John started feeling uncomfortable. Something didn't seem right. Unsure of what to do, he confided in his mother. That decision changed everything.

His parents immediately recognized the warning signs of a scam. But instead of reacting on impulse, they took a calculated approach. His father took over the conversation, pretending to be John, and agreed to send more money. At the same time, he contacted local law enforcement and provided them with transaction details from the Cash App payments.

The police traced the account to a 26-year-old man in another state with a history of online fraud. With the transaction records and online communication logs, authorities were able to track him down and make an arrest. He was charged with fraud, online exploitation, and attempting to solicit money from a minor.

Cyberbullying and Harassment

Cyberbullying does not end when a child leaves school; it can persist 24/7 through social media, messaging apps, gaming platforms, and other digital spaces. It isn't just about being mean. It can include hurtful comments and social exclusion to more severe forms such as doxxing, threats, and public humiliation.

How cyberbullying and harassment work?

Kids' social lives are tightly connected to their digital world and social media accounts, so when someone targets them publicly, it can feel like their entire world is turning against them.

Here's how cyberbullying typically shows up:

Rumors and lies: Bullies post false or damaging information about their victims to embarrass or socially isolate them. From embarrassing stories, fake screenshots, or twisted versions of real events, the goal is to damage the victim's reputation and make others turn away from them.

Impersonation: Harassers create fake profiles impersonating the victim. They use these accounts to post offensive content or message others in a way that gets the real child blamed or judged, sometimes even by family and friends.

Trolling: Some bullies troll, posting provocative or offensive messages to trigger emotional reactions and ridicule their target. It might be something cruel, mocking, or deeply personal. The idea is to get the victim upset while others watch, laugh, or join in.

Threats: In severe cases, the messages go beyond teasing. Bullies send direct threats of harm, causing psychological distress to their victims.

Exclusion: Bullies deliberately exclude individuals from online groups, chats, or activities to make them feel isolated and rejected. The bullies make sure the child knows they're being left out, using it as a form of social punishment.

True story: How a parent's vigilance saved their child

Cyberbullying can take many forms. A few years ago, the teenage daughter of an acquaintance of mine became the target of online harassment that threatened her reputation and well-being.

Carla was in ninth grade when it all happened. It wasn't sudden or dramatic at first. It started with small things, friends stopped including her in group projects, people in class glanced at her and whispered, and her usual lunch group drifted away. She noticed that her classmates, who were once her good friends, started avoiding her but wouldn't tell her why.

What Carla didn't know was that someone had created a fake Instagram profile in her name. This impersonator had posted hurtful comments about classmates, making it appear that Carla was bullying others. Because the account used her real name and photos, many students at her school wrongly believed that Carla was responsible. As a result, she faced social exclusion, hostility, and emotional distress without understanding why.

Carla's parents began to notice the changes at home. She became withdrawn and less focused. She stopped doing the things she used to love, and her grades slipped. She seemed exhausted all the time but never wanted to talk about it. Instead of brushing off these signs as something that accompanies adolescence, her parents initiated an open and non-judgmental conversation. Through this discussion, Carla revealed her suspicions about classmates treating her differently.

Her parents, one of whom was a cybersecurity professional, intuitively went online to check Carla's social media accounts and emails. They searched her name online, leading them to discover the fake profile impersonating their daughter.

Due to their swift action, the fake account was removed. Soon after, the school identified and disciplined the cyberbully. But the real win was that Carla recovered emotionally. Her parents listened carefully and believed her without question, and the school offered steady support. Over time, Carla reconnected with her friends, explained the reality, and slowly regained her confidence.

Sextortion and Blackmail

Sextortion and blackmail are serious online threats that prey on fear, shame, and coercion. Sextortion occurs when a predator or cybercriminal obtains explicit images, videos, or personal information and then threatens to distribute them unless the victim complies with their demands. These demands can include sending more images, engaging in explicit acts, or providing money or personal details.

How sextortion and blackmail work?

For anybody, the emotional fallout that sextortion brings can be overwhelming. Shame, fear, and panic often keep the victims from reaching out for help. That's exactly what predators count on. The best defense against this crime is awareness, open communication, and educating children on recognizing and avoiding these manipulative tactics.

Initial contact: Predators initiate contact through public forums, gaming platforms, or messaging apps, sometimes posing as someone the victim's age. They initiate casual conversation and try to build a connection quickly.

Grooming: The predator carefully builds trust, making the victim feel safe enough to share personal or explicit content.

Capturing explicit content: The criminal convinces the victim to send compromising photos or videos, often using flattery, deception, or false promises. The goal is to get the victim to send compromising photos or videos, with the requests often normalized with "*just between us*" or "*something couples do.*"

Threats and coercion: Once the predator has the content, everything changes. They threaten to post it publicly unless the victim sends more material, pays money, or follows certain demands. The victim is terrified of being exposed and often feels stuck.

Continued exploitation: Sextortion rarely ends with one demand. Once the predator gains leverage, they escalate. They use guilt, fear, and shame to keep the victim quiet and compliant. It becomes a cycle that's emotionally exhausting and psychologically damaging.

True story: How a 15-year-old escaped the trap

A close personal friend of mine has a 15-year-old daughter whom we'll call Emma. Emma was an ordinary teenager who loved Instagram. She was what her peers would call an "*Instagirl.*" She loved chatting with friends and making new connections online. She'd post outfit selfies, dance trends, and snippets from her day.

One afternoon, she got a DM from a new follower. His profile showed a teenage boy around her age, with a casual bio and photos that made him seem like someone she'd probably go to school with if he lived nearby. He said he'd found her account through a mutual hashtag and liked her "vibe." The conversation started light, comments about music, favorite shows, memes. He was polite, funny, and just flirty enough to feel exciting but not uncomfortable.

Over the next few weeks, they chatted every day. He'd ask how her day at school was, tell her she was beautiful, and say things like *"You're different from other girls on here."* To a 15-year-old, that kind of attention feels validating. Emma grew to trust him. Eventually, he asked if sending her a risqué photo would be OK. He asked her to return one when she'd received it, reassuring her it was between them. The moment she sent the image, everything changed.

The tone of the messages changed utterly. Instead of warm, supportive messages, she started receiving cold, threatening messages. The predator revealed that he had saved the photo and would expose her if she didn't comply with his demands. He demanded more explicit images or a sum of money, warning that if she refused, he would send the picture to her family, friends, and schoolmates.

Emma was terrified. She felt trapped and ashamed, afraid of what might happen if her parents or classmates found out. She blocked him, hoping that would make it stop. But the messages didn't stop. He created new accounts and kept coming back, each time more aggressive. He sent screenshots of her friends' profiles, making it clear he had done his research. After about two weeks of enduring this blackmail, Emma finally broke down and told her parents everything.

Her parents sat with her and listened without judgment. They assured her she wasn't in trouble. They collected every message and screenshot, carefully documenting everything. Then they reported the blackmail to Meta, the parent company of Instagram, and the local police.

The sheriff's department had a cybercrime unit that took the case seriously. Officers came to their home to walk them through the next steps, offering both investigative support and emotional resources. They helped connect Emma with a counselor trained to work with teens affected by online abuse.

Over time, the messages stopped. Authorities traced the IP addresses behind the fake accounts and opened an investigation. Emma didn't get full closure right away, but she got something just as important, safety, support, and a path toward healing.

Online Gaming Scams

Online gaming can be a lot of fun for kids, but it has also become a hotspot for scams and predatory behavior. Online gaming scams exploit players' desire for in-game rewards, social status, or excitement.

How gaming scams work?

Fake in-game items: Scammers offer rare skins, weapons, or virtual currency to trick players into sending money or account details. Once the payment is made, the scammer vanishes.

Phishing links: Scammers send links that look like promotions or giveaways, *"You've unlocked an exclusive outfit!"* or *"Claim your free coins here."* These direct the victim to fake login pages designed to steal account details.

Malicious software: Some sites promise cheat codes or hacks to help players win in a popular game. But these downloads often install malware behind the scenes. Once a malware infects a device, it can steal personal information, spy on activity, or hijack gaming accounts.

Account hijacks: Scammers pose as game moderators or trusted players, asking for login credentials *"to fix an issue."* Once inside the account, they change the password, lock the child out, and demand money to give it back. Some don't even want money; they just do it for control.

Grooming: Predators use in-game chats to befriend children, coercing them into sharing personal information or even engaging in inappropriate behavior.

True Story: The Lucknow Gaming Scam

In late August 2024, a middle-class family living in Indiranagar, Lucknow, India, found themselves at the center of a disturbing cybercrime involving their 12-year-old son. A Class 7 student and avid online gamer, the boy had fallen prey to a scammer posing as a gaming expert, one who promised access to exclusive game levels and premium rewards.

What began as playful curiosity soon spiraled into manipulation and deception. The scammer, identified by police as Prakash Mehrana, used common grooming tactics tailored to children's online behavior. Through direct chats and in-game messages, he convinced the boy that to unlock certain elite features in the game, he would need to make real-money payments. He made it sound like a limited-time opportunity: "Act now or lose your chance forever." Desperate to win and earn in-game prestige, the child complied.

Unbeknownst to his parents, the boy had access to their mobile devices and online banking apps. Over an 11-day period, from August 24 to September 4, he transferred a staggering ₹5 lakh (approximately $6,000 USD) to Mehrana's account. The money was taken in chunks: ₹2.3 lakh from his mother's account and ₹2.59 lakh from his father's. No alerts were raised initially, as the scammer instructed the boy on how to erase transaction histories and mute notification messages.

The crime came to light when the mother reviewed her monthly bank statement and discovered several suspicious withdrawals. Shocked and alarmed, the family questioned their son, who broke down and confessed the truth.

They immediately contacted the Indiranagar police. With assistance from the cybercrime unit, the police traced the transactions and registered a First Information Report (FIR) against Mehrana. A formal investigation is ongoing.

Psychologist Manini Srivastava, consulted during the case, explained how digital gratification can distort a child's sense of reality and responsibility. "Children are particularly vulnerable to the promise of instant rewards," she said. "In a game, when you spend tokens or coins, the impact isn't real. So when scammers ask for real money, many kids don't grasp what they're giving away."

This incident underscores a critical issue: children are no longer just passive consumers of digital media; they're active participants in a complex online ecosystem that includes gaming, chat, digital wallets, and microtransactions. And in many cases, parents are unaware of just how financially and emotionally immersive those platforms can be.

The Lucknow gaming scam is a sobering reminder for families everywhere. Even a smart, well-adjusted child can be targeted and manipulated by someone who understands the psychology of gaming and reward.

Malware and Spyware Attacks

Malware, short for malicious software, refers to any program that's designed to mess with your device or steal your information. It includes viruses, spyware, ransomware, and other stuff you don't want anywhere near your phone, tablet, or laptop.

How malware works?

Infected downloads: Malware hides in files that look safe: free games, "mods," pirated software, or even homework tools. Once downloaded, the malware installs itself quietly in the background and can start stealing data or slowing down the device.

Phishing links in emails: Clicking on links in fake emails or social media messages can install malware without the user's knowledge.

Sketchy ads and pop-ups: Some websites are loaded with ads that scream things like *"Your phone is infected!"* or *"Congratulations! You just won $9999"* Clicking them can trigger automatic malware downloads or redirect the user to a fake antivirus page that asks for payment info.

Keyloggers and spyware: This type of malware captures everything you do on your device, from search history, passwords, and personal data. It's designed to be invisible, which makes it even more dangerous if it lands on a device your child uses for school or social media.

Ransomware: It locks the user out of their files or sometimes the entire device, and demands a ransom to "unlock" it. Once it's in, there's often no easy fix.

True story: Matt's Costly Click

Matt, an 11-year-old boy from California, loved playing Roblox. He spent hours designing his worlds, trading virtual items, and chatting with other players. He wasn't the type to think much about online security, after all, he was just playing games.

One evening, while playing a popular Roblox game, Matt

received a chat message from another player. The message read:

"Hey, I saw your avatar and thought you might want some free Robux! I just found a promo site that gives loads of extra game credits. It worked for me!! Check it out."

Thoroughly excited by this "rare opportunity," Matt clicked the link. The website that opened looked exactly like Roblox's official page. Matt typed in his username and password, just as usual, and waited to "claim the reward." The site refreshed a couple of times, and a generic error message popped up. Matt assumed the offer was a glitch or fake, so he shrugged it off and returned to playing.

What Matt didn't know at the time was that he had unknowingly downloaded a malicious file onto his tablet. The malware quietly entered his family's home network.

The following morning, Matt's parents woke up to a nightmare. His mother's phone was flooded with banking alerts:

$4,200 transferred to an unknown overseas account.

Multiple credit card charges for online purchases.

A new loan application submitted under Matt's dad's name.

Confused and panicked, Matt's dad tried logging in to his bank account, but his password had been changed. The parents immediately contacted the bank and froze all accounts to stop further losses. They also called their internet provider, fearing a hack on their Wi-Fi network.

An IT specialist was brought in to investigate. After scanning the devices, he found the source of the attack and mitigated the threat. But the malware had already spread to the corporate laptops, personal phones, and tablets, all of which were connected to the home network. A simple Roblox chat message led to a serious financial disaster.

Social Media Exploitation and Fake Influencers

On the surface, social media looks like a space for fun and self-expression. Underneath, it's rife with people and systems designed to influence behavior, collect data, and misuse trust for profit. Scammers, fake influencers, and even some real ones use carefully curated content to push products that *"they just love,"* gain followers or *"fam,"* or convince viewers to *"support an important cause"* by sending money.

How social media exploitation works?

Fake influencers: Creating a convincing influencer profile is becoming increasingly easy. All it takes is a curated profile and a few borrowed lifestyle shots. With the right hashtags and posts, these accounts can appear highly real. Such fake influencers sell a dream, a lavish lifestyle, miracle products, or "easy money" schemes, pressuring kids to engage with content that's misleading, risky, or outright fraudulent.

Phony giveaways: Children are lured in with promises of free gadgets, gift cards, or exclusive perks. To enter, they're asked to share personal info, follow accounts, or tag friends, unknowingly helping spread the scam.

Financial exploitation: Some social media figures encourage children to spend money on unnecessary subscriptions, donate to unreal causes, or buy into "limited-time" schemes. Phrases like *"support your favorite creator"* or *"don't miss out"* help bypass rational thinking and trigger impulse behavior in viewers.

Data mining: Several social platforms, including the most popular ones, track and store every click and every scroll. Children's data is incredibly valuable and often collected without clear consent.

Social pressure: Algorithms reward popularity, appearance, and engagement. In an effort to keep up, children increasingly incline toward the curated lifestyle of the influencers. The unrealistic standards lead to anxiety, low self-worth, and risky behavior.

True story: Hola amigo!

Nick was obsessed with social media. Like many teens, he followed his favorite influencers religiously. He kept up with their latest gaming tips, giveaways, and lifestyle updates. His biggest idol was a famous YouTuber and Twitch streamer known for his engaging gaming content and generous giveaways, whom we will call Sandro.

Nick had always dreamed of interacting with Sandro. So when he received a direct message on Instagram from an account named @sandro_official, his heart skipped a beat. The message read:

"¡Hola, amigo! You've been randomly selected for my VIP giveaway! I'm picking 50 lucky fans to win gaming gear and a $500 gift card. All you have to do is pay a small $25 shipping fee, and it's yours!"

Nick was thrilled. This was his chance to get noticed by his idol AND score a considerable prize. The account looked legitimate; it had Sandro's profile picture, a bio that matched his real account, and thousands of followers. Without hesitation, Nick replied:

"Wow! Thank you so much, Sandro! How do I pay?"

The scammer who impersonated the YouTuber sent him a payment link through a third-party site. It looked official enough, and Nick eagerly entered the debit card details he had borrowed from his mother. Minutes later, he received a confirmation message:

"Felicidades! Your VIP package will arrive in 5–7 business days. Stay tuned for more exclusive giveaways!"

Excited, Nick told his mom about the giveaway, already picturing the expensive gaming headset and gift card he'd soon receive. But his excitement faded a few days later when he checked Sandro's real Instagram page and saw a warning post:

" ¡CUIDADO! Someone is impersonating me and messaging fans! I NEVER ask for payments for giveaways! Please report any fake accounts! Stay safe!"

Nick's stomach dropped. He immediately checked the profile

that had messaged him, but it was gone already. He tried to contact the payment site but there was no customer service. His $25 was gone, and worse, he had entered the debit card details into a scam website.

On checking Nick's mother's bank account, the family found multiple unauthorized transactions, including a $150 purchase for cryptocurrency and $90 spent on unknown digital services. His mother immediately froze the account and disputed the charges.

While they recovered some of the stolen money, Nick's family lost $75 in fraudulent transactions before the scammers disappeared. The experience left Nick feeling embarrassed and betrayed. He couldn't believe he had been tricked so easily.

Deepfake and AI-Based Attacks

Deepfake and AI-based attacks use advanced AI systems and image generation engines to create audio, images, or videos that look and sound completely real. These attacks mess with emotions, memories, and even relationships.

How deepfake and AI-based attacks work

Fake videos and audio: AI-driven deepfake technology can alter videos or create entirely fabricated footage, making it appear that someone said or did something they never actually did. This can be used for cyberbullying, blackmail, or misinformation.

Synthetic identity: Criminals use AI-generated fake identities to commit fraud, apply for credit, loans, or accounts in someone else's name.

Voice-mimicking scams: Attackers use AI to mimic the voice of someone your child trusts. The scammer might call and ask for private information or say there's an emergency, tricking the child into sharing things they normally wouldn't.

Deepfake blackmail: Cybercriminals create compromising but entirely fake images or videos of a victim and threaten to share them unless a demand is met, a form of digital extortion that preys on fear and shame.

Misinformation: Deepfakes are used to impersonate public figures, making them appear to say or do things that fuel confusion, fear, or controversy.

AI chatbots and autonomous manipulators: With the rise of AI tools like Replika, Character.ai, and other roleplay bots, children are engaging in long, emotional conversations with AI-generated personas. This opens doors to new forms of grooming, manipulation, or ideological influence.

True Story: AI Abuse at a Pennsylvania High School

In early 2024, Lancaster Country Day School, a prestigious private institution in Pennsylvania, found itself at the center of one of the most alarming digital exploitation cases in recent U.S. history. The incident didn't involve hacking or stolen passwords, it involved artificial intelligence. Specifically, the misuse of AI-powered image generation to create fake explicit content targeting real students.

Two male students, both minors at the time, were arrested and charged after it was discovered that they had used AI applications to manipulate images of their female classmates. The apps, available freely online, allowed users to upload ordinary social media photos and render them into disturbingly realistic nude images. These altered pictures were then shared with other students via Discord, a popular communication platform often used for gaming and private chat groups.

What began as a quiet investigation quickly escalated when school officials and law enforcement realized the scale of the incident. In total, nearly 500 criminal charges were filed against the boys, including counts of child pornography production, possession, distribution, and criminal use of a communication facility. The number of identified victims reached 60, with 48 of them being students currently enrolled at Lancaster Country Day. The other victims included students from nearby schools or girls whose photos were accessible through public platforms.

Parents, teachers, and the local community were horrified, not just by the scope of the exploitation, but by how it was done. These were not stolen photographs or screenshots from private accounts. These were AI-generated images created without the victims' knowledge or consent, based on everyday selfies, group pictures, or school portraits pulled from Instagram and Snapchat.

As news spread, it became clear this wasn't an isolated

case. The rise of AI-powered "nudify" tools, some marketed as entertainment, others hiding behind anonymity, has introduced an insidious form of image-based abuse. The fact that these tools are accessible to anyone with a smartphone and no technical skills required makes them particularly dangerous in the hands of teenagers.

Law enforcement officials involved in the case emphasized that the legal system is still catching up. "We're seeing criminal behavior that couldn't have existed even five years ago," said one of the prosecutors. "And the emotional harm to the victims is very real, many of them feel violated, shamed, and unsafe, even though the images weren't physically real."

The school responded by offering counseling to affected students and implementing stricter digital conduct policies. However, the damage had already been done. Some victims reported being harassed by peers who had seen the images, while others simply stopped attending school altogether.

Swatting

Swatting is a dangerous form of cyber harassment in which someone makes a false report to emergency services, prompting a heavily armed police response to a victim's home. The goal of the perpetrator is to cause fear, confusion, and, in some cases, physical harm to the victim.

Swatting is commonly associated with online gaming and social media conflicts, but anyone can be targeted.

How swatting works?

Swatting is a dangerous prank and potentially a deadly cybercrime. It exploits emergency response systems and puts both victims and law enforcement at risk. Victims of swatting may suffer emotional trauma, property damage, or even physical harm due to the aggressive police response.

Here's how swatting typically works:

Collecting personal information: Swatters gather a victim's address and personal details through doxxing, social engineering, or data leaks.

A hoax emergency call: The attacker calls emergency services, falsely reporting a serious threat such as a hostage situation, bomb threat, or active shooter at the victim's address.

Triggering a SWAT response: Law enforcement, believing the threat to be accurate, dispatches a SWAT team or other emergency responders to the location.

Publicizing the attack: Sometimes, swatters stream the incident online or share it within their online communities to harass, intimidate, or embarrass the victim.

True Story: A $1.50 Wager and a Life Lost

In December 2017, a petty argument over a $1.50 wager in an online video game spiraled into a tragic event that cost an innocent man his life and changed the course of several others. What began as typical online trash talk between three gamers:

Casey Viner, Tyler Barriss, and Shane Gaskill, escalated into one of the most high-profile examples of this type of attack.

In this case, Viner and Gaskill had been arguing over the outcome of a match in the game *Call of Duty*. In a moment of anger, Viner contacted Barriss, a known swatter with a history of making false emergency calls. Viner asked Barriss to "hit" Gaskill by calling in a fake police report.

Barriss made the call to Wichita, Kansas police, falsely claiming that a man at a certain address had killed his father and was holding his family hostage. He gave the 911 dispatcher an address that had once belonged to Gaskill, but Gaskill no longer lived there.

When officers arrived at the address, they encountered Andrew Finch, a 28-year-old father of two who had no connection to the online dispute. He stepped outside onto his porch to see what was happening and, in the confusion and tension of the moment, was fatally shot by police. Finch had done nothing wrong. He wasn't involved in gaming, swatting, or the argument. He was simply in the wrong place at the wrong time.

The tragedy prompted national outrage and brought attention to the real-life dangers of online revenge culture. It also highlighted a critical lack of legal precedent for crimes committed through virtual actions.

Following the investigation:

- Casey Viner pleaded guilty to conspiracy and obstruction of justice. He was sentenced to 15 months in prison, followed by a two-year ban from gaming.

- Tyler Barriss, the swatter who made the false call, pleaded guilty to 51 federal charges, including making false reports, cyberstalking, and causing a death through false information. He was sentenced to 20 years in federal prison.

- Shane Gaskill, who had given out his old address and dared Viner to "do something about it," later pleaded guilty to wire fraud and was sentenced to 18 months in prison.

This case remains one of the most chilling reminders of how online actions can have devastating offline consequences. For parents and children alike, it underscores why digital conflicts—especially in gaming environments—must never be taken lightly. A single impulsive message, a moment of rage, or an attempt at a 'joke' can destroy lives.

Chapter 3

Recognizing Online Threats

While the previous chapter outlined the many types of online threats your child may encounter, this chapter will guide you on how to recognize the warning signs that your child may be at risk.

Online threats don't always present themselves in obvious ways. A child being targeted by cybercriminals, predators, or online bullies may not openly share their experiences, making it crucial for parents to be proactive. Learn how to recognize changes in behavior, patterns in online activity, and red flags that indicate potential danger.

Also, children might not always realize when they are being manipulated or exploited. So, as parents and caregivers, we must stay vigilant.

Sudden secrecy about online activity

Many children worry that they will be punished or lose access to their devices if they admit they have engaged with a scammer, shared personal information, or been deceived. To add to this, scammers and predators often convince children that their parents *"won't understand"* or that seeking help will make things worse.

If your child suddenly becomes secretive about their digital life, it could be a sign that something online is making them uncomfortable or that they're involved in interactions they know you wouldn't approve of.

Secrecy can take many forms. Some telltale signs are:

- Minimizing or closing screens the moment someone walks into the room.
- Frequently deleting messages and browsing history.
- Avoiding conversations about online activities.
- Preferring to use devices in private.

These behaviors can be a red flag for several types of online threats. You need to understand that children may feel embarrassed, scared, or even threatened by someone online, making them withdraw rather than seek help. While not every change signals danger, consistent patterns of secrecy are worth paying attention to.

Children tricked or manipulated online may feel ashamed of their actions and fear judgment from their parents or peers. Older children and teenagers, in particular, may believe that they can resolve the issue without adult intervention, not realizing the full extent of the danger.

Unexplained financial transactions or missing money

One of the most overlooked—but significant—warning signs that a child may be involved in an online scam is unexplained financial activity. Scammers use psychological manipulation, making victims feel obligated, guilty, or rushed into making transactions. Some even impersonate authority figures or use fear tactics to pressure children into compliance.

Children may not realize they have been scammed until it's too late. Because they fear getting in trouble, they attempt to cover up the situation rather than ask for help. Recognizing these warning signs early can prevent further financial loss and protect your child from future scams.

Signs of ongoing financial exploitation include:

- Unfamiliar transactions, subscriptions, or in-game purchases on your or your family's bank statement or linked credit cards.
- Disappearing gift cards or digital currency stored in your e-wallets.
- Requests for money from online "friends."
- Your child mentioning job offers or online gigs that are just too good to be true.
- Your child suddenly expressing curiosity about online investing, cryptocurrency, or stocks with little prior knowledge.
- Missing cash or physical valuables.

Emotional distress and anxiety

Another critical warning sign that a child may be experiencing online threats is a noticeable increase in emotional distress or anxiety. While emotional ups and downs are normal, persistent signs of stress may indicate they are facing cyberbullying, harassment, or other online dangers.

Indicators of emotional distress linked to online threats include:

- Sudden mood swings with your child becoming easily irritated, withdrawn, or unusually aggressive.
- Inexplicable avoidance of online activity, where a child who once enjoyed playing games, using social media, or chatting with friends suddenly shows reluctance to go online.
- Changes in sleep patterns, insomnia, frequent nightmares, or excessive sleeping as an escape mechanism.
- Loss of interest in hobbies.
- Frequent headaches, stomachaches, and other stress-related ailments caused by prolonged anxiety.
- Social withdrawal and isolation from friends and family.

Recognizing emotional distress early can help parents intervene before online threats escalate. Understanding the root cause and fostering an open dialogue with your child is key to ensuring their emotional well-being and digital safety.

Receiving unsolicited messages from strangers

One of the most precise indicators that your child may be at risk online is receiving unsolicited messages from strangers. These messages can come from various platforms, including social media, online gaming, email, and messaging apps. While some may appear harmless, others can be the starting point for scams, grooming, cyberbullying, or exploitation.

Unsolicited messages include:

- Random friend requests or direct messages from people your child doesn't know in person.
- Overly friendly or flattering messages or social media comments from strangers.
- Requests for photos, especially personal or private ones.
- Invitations to join private chats, servers, or platforms outside the app.
- Messages that create urgency or fear, like threats or fake emergencies.
- Promises of prizes, money, or exclusive content in exchange for clicks or information.

Children don't always recognize the risks associated with such messages, especially if the sender appears friendly or trustworthy. While not every message from a stranger is inherently dangerous, children should be taught to be wary of any unsolicited contact.

Requests for personal information

We teach children not to talk to strangers in real life, but online, that rule can get blurry. When someone starts asking questions, it often feels like a normal "getting to know you" conversation. And because kids are taught to be polite and friendly, they tend to answer without realizing that these questions may be part of a scammer's strategy to gather personal information.

Common information they try to collect includes:

- A child's full name, age, or location
- School name, daily routine, or places they spend time
- Phone number or email to shift the conversation off-platform
- Passwords or login info, often under the pretense of helping
- Details about family members, like parents' names or jobs
- Credit card or payment information in exchange for fake prizes or upgrades

Sudden obsession with earning online rewards

A growing trend among children and teenagers is the intense pursuit of online rewards, such as virtual currency, gaming perks, or exclusive digital items. While rewards can be a fun incentive in games and online activities, an excessive or sudden obsession with earning them may indicate that your child is engaging in potentially harmful or exploitative schemes.

Signs that your child may be caught in a risky or manipulative reward system include:

- Spending long hours glued to a screen and fixated on unlocking new perks, even at the expense of schoolwork, sleep, or time with friends
- Completing sketchy surveys or watching suspicious ads.
- Showing unusual frustration, anxiety, or mood swings when they can't reach a reward or are asked to put down their device.
- Starting asking for a few dollars here and there for in-game purchases, loot boxes, or "limited-time" offers.
- Repeatedly asking for gift cards instead of traditional gifts or allowances.
- Unexplained charges for virtual currency, digital goods, or in-game upgrades.
- Using gift cards to pay for online interactions or offers.
- Expressing sudden interest in trading or selling gift cards online.

These activities open the door to malware, phishing, and exploitation without the child realizing they've done anything risky. If your child seems unusually anxious or upset when they fall short of a reward goal, or if they start acting out when asked to take a break, the pressure they're feeling may not be about the game, it may be about something they can't quite name.

Fear of losing online accounts or access

Many children and teens develop a deep attachment to their online accounts. While enjoying and valuing online experiences is normal, an excessive fear of losing access to these accounts may signal underlying issues.

Signs of excessive fear of account loss include:

- Frequently worrying about getting locked out of an account.
- Repeatedly losing access to an account or getting locked out.
- Expression of extreme distress over the possibility of losing access to a specific game or platform.
- Being overly secretive about login details, passwords, or security settings.

Scammers, hackers, and online predators often use threats of account loss as leverage to manipulate children into complying with demands, sharing personal information, or even sending money. Recognizing when account security anxiety becomes a sign of online exploitation is key to protecting your child's digital well-being.

Drastic changes in online behavior

Teenagers change; it's part of growing up. Gradual changes in behavior are regular as children grow and develop new interests. It's quite natural for them to become more private, spend more time online, or be deeply invested in digital spaces like games, chats, or social media. However, there's a line between typical teenage behavior and signs that something more serious may be going on.

Experts in adolescent development agree that when behavioral changes are gradual and follow a pattern, such as shifting from one game to another, or spending more time texting friends, that's usually nothing to worry about. But sudden, intense, or extreme shifts may indicate that a child is experiencing something that they don't know how to manage or explain.

These shifts are often the first visible symptoms of a cyber threat. Here are some behaviors to keep an eye on:

- A sudden increase in screen time, especially late at night or away from shared spaces.
- Withdrawal from devices and online spaces they previously enjoyed.
- Defensive, evasive, or angry responses when asked about what they're doing online.
- Noticeable mood changes like sadness, frustration, or anxiety after using the internet.
- Habits such as hiding screens, switching accounts, or constantly changing passwords.

Individually, these behaviors could be minor. But together, they point to an ongoing issue your child may not yet have words for. Staying observant and approachable during such a time can make all the difference.

Changes in political or ideological beliefs

Not all online threats come in the form of scams or malware. Some show up more quietly, through changes in what your child believes, how they speak, or the content they start defending without question.

Sudden, rigid shifts in worldview especially when paired with strong emotional language, conspiracy talk, or intense "us vs. them" thinking can signal that your child is being influenced by online echo chambers.

The way it happens is rarely obvious. A child usually starts with a harmless interest which could be a documentary, a video essay, or a meme account. But social media algorithms are designed to feed more of what holds attention, not necessarily what's balanced. A video about government flaws on YouTube might lead to conspiracy content, which leads to long Reddit threads, which leads to Discord servers filled with older users who use sarcasm and inside jokes to build a sense of superiority. Some of these communities operate under a surface of humor, but their core messages promote hate, misinformation, or manipulation. Once inside, the feedback loop strengthens beliefs and discourages any outside perspective.

What makes this pipeline so effective is that it doesn't start with politics. It often begins with loneliness, boredom, or anger. A teen feeling isolated at school, disappointed by adults, or unsure about their identity may find comfort in strong-sounding messages and communities that offer belonging. These spaces often say, *"You see the truth that others don't."* That kind of praise can be deeply reassuring to a teen who is struggling. It builds a sense of superiority and belonging, which make the group feel more trustworthy than family or school.

You might notice your child becoming unusually hostile toward certain groups, mimicking internet jargon in everyday speech, or rejecting any opinion that doesn't match what they're seeing online. They tend to say things like, "You just believe what the media tells you," or dismiss teachers, family members, or peers as "NPCs." These are important signs of a closed feedback loop.

All this becomes a real cybersecurity threat when these communities push your child toward harmful actions. Some radicalized spaces encourage harassment campaigns, doxxing, or participation in illegal forums. Others promote the use of encrypted messaging apps to hide conversations, or trick teens into downloading "tools" that can be used for trolling or attacks, which may contain malware themselves. In extreme cases, young people can be groomed into spreading hate speech, coordinating swatting attacks, or participating in digital vandalism, thinking it's just "edgy" or "funny." What starts as ideological influence can become direct involvement in cybercrime.

If you notice this shift, resist the instinct to confront or criticize. Calling it out bluntly can backfire, making your child more defensive and more loyal to the online space that "gets them." Instead, ask questions. Be curious. Try:

"That's an interesting take. Where'd you come across that idea?"

"Do you think there's any part of the other side that makes sense?"

"How do you decide what's true when you see different opinions online?"

Your goal isn't to win a debate. It's to keep a line open. When kids feel they can talk without being judged, they're more likely to bring up things that concern them and more open to thinking critically.

Not every belief change is a red flag. Teens explore. They push boundaries. But when those changes come fast, are driven by anger or isolation, and show signs of online manipulation, it's worth stepping in.

CHAPTER 4

Securing Social Media Accounts

To ensure a safer online experience, parents and children need to understand platform-specific security measures and the best practices to be followed when kids introduce themselves to social media. This chapter provides detailed strategies to enhance security on children and teens' most popular social media platforms.

TikTok

TikTok is a short-form video-sharing app popular among young users. The videos are usually 15 to 60 seconds long. For many teens, TikTok is a space to be creative, follow trends, or feel part of a wider community. They post dance routines, comedy skits, reaction videos, or just everyday moments. The feedback loop of likes, views, and comments feels greatly rewarding and addicting.

The platform is public by default, which means strangers can view, comment, and message unless privacy settings are adjusted. Kids may also be exposed to inappropriate content. In some cases, videos intended for friends go viral, reaching an unintended and sometimes unsafe audience.

TikTok's ownership has recently raised concerns about data privacy and potential surveillance. The app collects extensive user data, including location, device information, and browsing habits, leading to scrutiny worldwide. Helping your child set up their TikTok account with privacy controls, limiting who can comment or message, and encouraging mindful posting are important steps in keeping their experience safe on this platform.

Privacy and safety settings:

Set the account to private

By default, TikTok accounts are public, allowing anyone to view the posted content. Setting the account to private ensures that only approved followers can see videos and interact.

1. To set account settings to Private:

    - Go to Settings & Privacy > Privacy.
    - Toggle Private Account ON.

Limiting who can send direct messages reduces the risk of inappropriate interactions and online grooming.

2. To Restrict Direct Message:

    - Go to Settings & Privacy > Privacy > Direct Messages.
    - Select No One or Friends Only (for approved followers).
    - Turn off message requests from unknown users.

Comments can expose children to cyberbullying and unwanted interactions. Restricting comments helps create a safer environment.

3. Control who can comment on videos

- Go to Settings & Privacy > Privacy > Comments.
- Choose Friends Only or No One.
- Enable Comment Filters to block offensive words and spam.

Duet and Stitch features allow strangers to use your child's videos to create new content, sometimes leading to misuse.

4. Disable Duet and Stitch features

- Go to Settings & Privacy > Privacy > Duet and Stitch.
- Set both to Friends Only or No One.

TikTok collects location data, which could put children at risk of being targeted or tracked.

5. Turn off location tracking

- Go to the device's Settings > Apps > TikTok.
- Disable Location Permissions.

Restricted Mode filters out inappropriate content and helps keep TikTok safe for children.

6. Enable Restricted Mode

- Go to Settings & Privacy > Content Preferences.

- Enable Restricted Mode.
- Set up a passcode to prevent children from changing this setting intentionally or unintentionally.

TikTok's Family Pairing feature allows parents to link their accounts to their child's, giving them control over privacy settings, screen time, and direct messages.

7. To set up Family Pairing

- Go to Settings & Privacy > Family Pairing.
- Follow the on-screen instructions to link accounts.

TikTok's addictive nature can lead to excessive screen time. Setting screen time limits helps balance usage.

8. Monitor screen time limits

- Go to Settings & Privacy > Digital Well-Being > Screen Time Management.
- Set daily limits and enable a passcode.

Instagram

Instagram is more than just a photo app. What draws many teens to this app is the ability to showcase their interests, whether it's art, sports, humor, or activism. Popular features like stories and reels let them share moments that disappear after a day, which feels more spontaneous and less permanent than a regular post.

But despite its polished surface, Instagram comes with a few hidden risks. Public accounts make it easy for strangers to view and interact with a teen's content. The pressure to maintain a perfect image can fuel anxiety or low self-esteem, especially when likes and comments become a measure of self-worth. Direct messages are sometimes misused for harassment, unsolicited contact, or scams.

While Instagram gives teens room to express and explore, it also makes it important for families to talk about boundaries, like thinking before posting, knowing how to block or report, and remembering that not everything online is as perfect as it looks.

Privacy and safety settings:

To help your child stay safe on Instagram, focus on three key areas: privacy, interaction control, and screen time. The steps below make the platform safer without taking away the freedom they value.

Limit visibility of your child's posts, profile, and followers to only approved connections.

1. Make the account private

- Go to Profile > ≡ Menu > Settings and Privacy > Account Privacy.
- Toggle Private Account on.

Filter who can contact your child, comment on posts, or view their stories and reels. For Direct Messages, set message access to trusted connections only.

2. Control interactions (DMs, Comments, and Tags)

- Go to Settings and Privacy > Messages and Story Replies.

- In Message Controls, choose "People You Follow" or "No One."

3. For Comments, prevent unwanted comments by limiting who can respond.

- Go to Settings and Privacy > Comments.
- Choose comment access or turn off per post.

4. For Stories/Reels, keep personal moments private by hiding stories from specific accounts.

- Go to Settings and Privacy > Stories and Reels.
- Hide Story and Reels From > Select users.

5. For restricting suspicious accounts, quietly reduce someone's ability to interact without blocking.

- Go to their profile > ••• Menu > Restrict.

Block unnecessary data collection, reduce tracking, and safeguard sensitive information. Stop the app from accessing or revealing physical locations.

6. Protect privacy and personal data

- Go to Phone Settings > Instagram App > Location > Set to "Never" or "Ask Every Time."
- Skip adding location info to posts and stories.
- Revoke access for connected apps your child doesn't use or recognize.

7. Manage screen time and digital well-being

Encourage healthy habits and reduce compulsive scrolling. Set a Daily Time Limit to cap usage. Enable Take a Break reminders at set intervals.

Snapchat

Snapchat is built for fast, casual communication; photos, videos, and messages may disappear after they're viewed. That's exactly what makes it so appealing to teens. It feels temporary, private, and spontaneous.

Teens use Snapchat to send selfies, keep streaks going with close friends, post short "Stories," and chat in group threads without leaving a visible record. But this sense of privacy can also be misleading. Messages may disappear on the surface, but screenshots, screen recordings, or third-party apps can still capture them.

Predators and scammers often take advantage of Snapchat's temporary nature to manipulate kids into engaging in risky behavior. Disappearing messages allow predators to pressure children into sharing personal information, images, or videos, making it difficult for parents or authorities to track conversations.

Another concern: the Snap Map feature shows a user's real-time location to friends unless it's turned off. If left on, it can expose your child's location to people they may not know well, or at all. The Quick Add feature can also surface your child's profile to strangers with mutual contacts, increasing the chance of unsolicited messages.

Privacy and safety settings:

Anyone can send messages to a user by default unless privacy settings are changed. Limiting contacts ensures that only known individuals can communicate with your child.

1. Limit who can contact your child

   - Go to Settings (gear icon in profile).
   - Tap Privacy Controls > Contact Me.
   - Select My Friends to ensure only approved friends can send Snaps or messages.

Snap Map can put children at risk of being tracked by strangers.

2. Enable Ghost Mode to disable location sharing

   - Go to Settings > Privacy Controls > See My Location.
   - Toggle Ghost Mode ON to prevent location tracking.

Snapchat Stories allows users to share photos and videos with followers, but strangers may be able to view and engage with them without restrictions.

3. Restrict who can view Stories

   - Go to Settings > Privacy Controls > View My Story.
   - Select My Friends or Custom to limit who can see posts.

If your child receives messages from unknown or inappropriate users, they should block and report those accounts immediately.

4. Block and report suspicious accounts

- Tap and hold the user's name.
- Select Manage Friendship > Block.
- If necessary, tap Report to notify Snapchat of inappropriate behavior.

Quick Add allows Snapchat to suggest new friends based on mutual contacts, which can expose your child to strangers.

5. Disable Quick Add

- Go to Settings > Privacy Controls > See Me in Quick Add.
- Toggle OFF.

A child's friends list should be reviewed regularly to ensure they are only connected with trusted individuals. Snapchat does not notify users when someone unfriends them.

6. Review friend lists regularly

- Open Snapchat, tap on the profile icon, then tap My Friends.
- Remove or block anyone unfamiliar or suspicious.

Snapchat's Discover section contains public stories, some of which may feature mature content. Restricting this feature helps prevent exposure to inappropriate media.

7. Filter out inappropriate content

- Go to Settings > Privacy Control > Family Center.

- Toggle on Restrict Sensitive Content.

YouTube

For many kids, teens, and adults, YouTube is the default destination when they're bored, curious, or trying to figure something out. It's also where they see people their age becoming famous, making money, or building loyal fanbases, all of which can make them want to post, comment, or participate more than they're ready for.

YouTube's algorithm is designed to keep viewers watching. It's not necessarily designed to keep them safe. Even with YouTube Kids and content filters, inappropriate videos still slip through. The comment sections often turn toxic, and some creators promote harmful ideas masked as humor or "edgy" content. There's also the growing trend of parasocial relationships, where kids feel emotionally connected to creators who don't know they exist, which can make them more easily influenced.

If your child posts content, they may also be exposed to unexpected feedback, ranging from praise to harassment. And because YouTube's reward system favors engagement and watch time, teens feel pressure to create content that's risky, exaggerated, or inauthentic just to keep up.

YouTube is vast, addictive, and filled with both valuable and questionable content. Helping your child understand how the platform works, why some videos rise to the top, and how to think critically about what they're watching or sharing is just as important as setting up content filters.

Privacy and safety settings:

YouTube Kids is a safer, more supervised version of YouTube that is designed for children. It provides filtered content, parental controls, and an ad-free experience.

1. Use YouTube Kids for younger viewers

    - Download the app from the app store
    - Set up an account with parental control settings
    - Choose the content level based on your child's age.

Restricted Mode helps block potentially inappropriate videos from appearing in your child's feed.

2. Enable Restricted Mode to filter out inappropriate content

    - Open the app and sign in to your child's account.
    - Click on the profile icon and select Settings.
    - Toggle Restricted Mode ON.

Autoplay can lead children to videos unrelated to their original search, sometimes exposing them to harmful or misleading content.

3. Disable Autoplay to prevent unintended content

    - Open YouTube and go to Settings.
    - Toggle Autoplay OFF.

If your child is uploading videos, turning off comments can prevent interactions with strangers and potential cyberbullying.

4. Turn off Comments on videos

- Sign in to YouTube Studio > Videos.
- In the left-hand menu, click on Content.
- Find the video you want to modify and click the pencil icon (Details) next to it.
- Scroll down and click on Show More to expand additional settings.
- Under the Comments and ratings section, locate the Comment visibility dropdown menu.
- Select Disable comments from the options.
- Click Save in the top-right corner to apply the changes.

If your child posts videos, limit who can view and interact with their content.

5. Limit who can interact with your child's content

- Go to YouTube Studio > Settings > Privacy.
- Set all videos to Private or Unlisted rather than Public.

Reviewing your child's watch history and the channels they subscribe to can help you detect inappropriate content.

6. Monitor Watch History and Subscriptions

- Open YouTube and go to Library > History.
- Discuss any concerning content with your child and adjust recommendations as needed.

For younger children, Google Family Link allows parents to control which apps and features their child can access, including YouTube.

7. Use Google Family Link to manage YouTube access

- Download the Google Family Link app
- Link your child's Google account and adjust YouTube permissions.

If your child encounters harmful content or inappropriate interactions, they should know how to report and block users.

8. Report and Block suspicious users and videos

- Tap the three-dot menu next to a video or comment.
- Select Report and choose the appropriate reason.
- Block the user if necessary.

Facebook

Facebook may seem like a platform today's teens have largely moved on from, but it's often required for school groups, family communication, or linked services like Instagram or gaming accounts. Teens also turn to Facebook for marketplace browsing, joining interest-based groups, or using Messenger to stay in touch with relatives or long-distance friends.

What makes Facebook unique is how much personal information it collects and displays by default: your child's birthday, location, schools, interests, and friend connections are all visible unless settings are changed. It also encourages ongoing engagement through notifications, memory prompts, event invites, and comment threads that can easily become public.

A growing concern is Facebook Marketplace scams, where fraudsters post fake listings for high-demand items, such as gaming consoles or limited-edition sneakers, luring teens into making payments for items that do not exist. Some scammers also request personal details under the guise of arranging transactions, potentially leading to identity theft. Additionally, predators use Marketplace to arrange unsafe meetups, putting young users at physical risk.

Privacy and safety settings:

Prevent strangers from accessing your child's posts, photos, and personal information.

1. Lock down profile visibility

    - Go to Settings & Privacy > Privacy Settings.
    - Under Who Can See Your Future Posts, select Friends Only.
    - Select Limit Past Posts to make previous public content visible to friends only.
    - Under Who Can See Your Posts, select Friends Only or use Custom Lists to exclude specific individuals.

- Under Do You Want Search Engines Outside Facebook to Link to Your Profile, select No.

Control who can contact your child and what personal info is publicly visible.

2. Limit connections and personal exposure

- Under Privacy Settings, set Who Can Send You Friend Requests to Friends of Friends.

- Go to Profile > About > Contact and Basic Info. Set visibility for phone number, email, birthday, and other sensitive info to Only Me or Friends.

Stop Facebook from sharing your child's location or tagging them in photos without consent.

3. Disable tracking and automatic tagging

- On your child's device, go to Settings > Apps > Facebook > Permissions, and disable Location Access.

- Avoid using or tagging locations in posts. Go to Settings & Privacy > Face Recognition. Set to No to turn off automatic photo tagging.

4. Secure Marketplace activity

- Teach your child how to navigate Facebook Marketplace safely. Avoid paying upfront; use in-person exchanges when possible. Check seller profiles and avoid those with limited info or reviews. Report fraudulent listings using the Report Listing option.

5. Block and Report suspicious activity

- Help your child know how to act when something doesn't feel right.
- On a post or profile, tap the three-dot menu.
- Select Report and follow the prompts.
- Use Block to prevent further messages or interactions.

Discord

Discord started as a group chat platform for gamers. Now, teens use it for everything from schoolwork and games to hobbies and private friend groups. It's organized around "servers," which are like group chats. Inside each server are channels for text, voice, and video.

Teens like Discord because it feels like their own space. They can talk in real time, connect with people who share their interests, and keep things more private than on apps like Instagram or TikTok. Some teens use it to study. Others use it to play, stream, or chat with friends late at night.

Discord servers are mostly public and easy to join. That means your child might end up talking to strangers. Some servers are poorly moderated. Others may contain adult content, toxic behavior, or people with bad intentions. Because Discord isn't based on a feed, what your child sees depends entirely on who they talk to and which servers they've joined.

Discord has privacy and safety settings, but many of them are turned off by default. Unwanted messages are also common in

Discord. Users can receive random friend requests or be added to unfamiliar servers. Some teens get pulled into inappropriate conversations without realizing it at first.

Privacy and safety settings:

By default, Discord lets anyone send your child a friend request or a direct message. Without adjusting privacy settings, it's easy for strangers to make contact or send inappropriate content.

1. Strengthen profile privacy and friend controls

- Go to User Settings > Privacy & Safety.
- Under Who Can Send You Friend Requests, deselect Everyone and select Friends of Friends or Server Members Only.
- Enable Keep Me Safe to automatically scan all direct messages for explicit or harmful content.
- Disable Allow Direct Messages from Server Members to prevent DMs from anyone in shared servers.

Even without public profiles, Discord users can be tracked based on activity, visible games, and linked accounts. These small data points reveal more than you expect.

2. Limit visibility and personal info sharing

- In Privacy & Safety, turn off Display current activity as a status message so strangers can't see what your child is doing or playing.
- In Connections, adjust the visibility of linked services like

Steam, Spotify, or Twitch. Set them to private.

- Encourage your child to use a nickname (not a real name) in servers.

- Consider changing their username and discriminator regularly to reduce traceability across servers.

Many Discord servers are public or loosely moderated. There are also bots which may introduce inappropriate features. Guide your child to join only those servers that they know or trust.

3. Control content and server access

- In any server they manage or participate in, review Server Settings > Roles to control permissions like who can message or invite.

- Enable Explicit Content Filtering under Privacy & Safety to automatically block inappropriate media.

- Regularly review and remove bots that aren't familiar or necessary.

Discord doesn't actively use GPS tracking, but indirect location sharing can still happen. Kids may mention where they live in chats, or third-party bots may ask for region-based information.

4. Minimize location-related risks

- Remind your child not to share location details in usernames, status messages, or server conversations.

- On mobile devices, go to the phone's settings > Discord App > Permissions, and turn off Location Access.

If your child is harassed, manipulated, or sent disturbing content, it's essential they know how to respond quickly.

5. Block and Report problematic users

- Right-click on the user's name or message.
- Select Report and choose the appropriate reason.
- Use Block to prevent further contact or visibility.

Roblox

Roblox is a platform filled with millions of games, most of them made by other users. Children can play games, build their own, customize avatars, and chat with other players. It feels creative, social, and open-ended, which is exactly what makes it so appealing and risky.

Roblox has built-in chat and in-game purchases, which means your child can be talking to strangers, seeing things you wouldn't expect in a kids' game, or spending money on virtual items without always understanding what they're doing. Some games look harmless but contain adult themes or unmoderated chat. And because anyone can create a game, even when moderation is present it isn't perfect.

There's also Robux, the platform's virtual currency. Kids use it to buy outfits, accessories, and game passes. But with peer influence and in-game status, the path can very easily lead to compulsive purchases or falling for scams.

The biggest misconception about Roblox is that it's safe because it's for kids. The reality is, it's only as safe as the settings you choose.

Roblox offers strong parental controls, but they're not automatic. You have to set them up.

Privacy and safety settings:

Roblox offers parental controls that limit content to age-appropriate experiences.

1. Filter games and content by age

- Go to Settings (gear icon) > Privacy.
- Toggle Account Restrictions ON to limit access to age-appropriate games.

Limiting online interactions helps reduce exposure to inappropriate messages and strangers.

2. Control who can message, chat, or join games

- Go to Settings > Privacy.
- Under Who Can Message Me, Who Can Chat With Me, and Who Can Join Me in Experiences, select Friends Only or No One.

Parents can set a PIN to prevent children from changing privacy and security settings.

3. Set a Parent PIN to lock privacy setting

- Go to Settings > Parental Controls.
- Create and confirm a Parent PIN to lock account settings.

Roblox uses Robux for in-game purchases, which can lead to unauthorized spending if not controlled.

4. Prevent unwanted Robux spending

- Make sure to monitor linked payment methods regularly and use prepaid Robux gift cards instead of credit or debit cards.
- Enable purchase notifications where possible.

Children may accept friend requests from strangers or enter questionable games.

5. Review friend list and recent game activity

- Go to the Friends tab.
- Remove unfamiliar contacts by selecting Unfriend.
- Check Recent Activity under your child's profile to review games played.

Parents need to check what games their child plays and block users engaging in inappropriate behavior.

6. Report inappropriate content or behavior

- Click the menu on a game or user profile.
- Select Report Abuse and follow the prompts provided.

X (Formerly Twitter)

Twitter, now rebranded as X, is a widely used microblogging platform. X isn't where most kids start their social media journey, but by the time they're teens, a lot of them end up there. Some use it to follow creators, meme pages, or fan accounts. Others use it to post anonymously, discuss pop culture, or vent. In many ways, it's built for broadcasting rather than connection.

Unlike Instagram or Snapchat, where users mostly talk to friends, X is about being seen by an audience. Teens post into a massive public feed where anyone can read, react, and repost. This public-by-default design means even a casual post can attract attention from people outside a user's immediate circle.

X also exposes users to a wide variety of content, including news, opinion threads, entertainment, and trending conversations. Because the platform relies heavily on real-time engagement, users may encounter sensitive or unmoderated content through trending topics, replies, or reposts. The "For You" feed curates content based on interaction and popularity, which may include material that isn't filtered by age unless specific settings are applied.

Privacy and safety settings:

Public posts can reach anyone on X. Restricting visibility and replies helps protect privacy and reduce unwanted interaction.

1. Control post visibility and replies

    - Go to Settings and privacy > Privacy and safety > Audience and tagging.

    - Toggle on Protect your posts.

2. To restrict who can reply to posts:

    - When composing a post, tap the reply settings icon.

- Select People you follow or Only people you mention.

X allows users to receive messages or requests from people they don't follow unless this is limited.

3. Manage direct messages and interaction

- Go to Settings and privacy > Privacy and safety > Direct messages.
- Turn off Allow message requests from everyone.

X includes an option to filter explicit media and mute words or topics that may be disturbing or inappropriate.

4. Limit exposure to sensitive or unwanted content

- Go to Settings and privacy > Privacy and safety > Content you see.
- Uncheck Display media that may contain sensitive content.
- To mute specific words or phrases:
- Go to Settings and privacy > Privacy and safety > Mute and block > Muted words.
- Tap Add, type in a word or phrase, and select how long and where to mute it.

Location data and public interaction history can reveal more than intended. Disabling these features adds another layer of protection.

5. Turn off location and limit profile visibility

- Go to Settings and privacy > Privacy and safety > Location information.
- Turn off Add location information to your posts.

6. To review and manage public activity:

- Go to your kid's profile.
- Review posts under Likes, Replies, and Posts to remove anything unintended.

Blocking or reporting helps your child stop unwanted interactions and flag harmful behavior directly to the platform.

7. Report inappropriate content or behavior

- Tap the three-dot icon on the user's profile or next to a post.
- Select Block or Report, then follow the instructions.

Pinterest

Unlike other social media platforms focusing on direct messaging and status updates, Pinterest operates more like a visual search engine, allowing users to browse, pin, and share images.

Pinterest may seem like a harmless and creative platform filled with DIY projects, fashion ideas, recipes, and aesthetic inspiration, but it isn't as safe as it appears, especially for children. Without proper safety measures, children can be exposed to inappropriate content, predators, and scams that disguise themselves as innocent images or links.

Privacy and safety settings:

Pinterest accounts are public by default, and anyone can view boards, pins, or follow the user unless visibility is limited.

1. Set the account to private via search and visibility

- Go to Settings > Privacy and data.
- Toggle off Allow search engines to include your profile.
- Make sure personal details (bio, links) are minimal or non-identifying.

Pinterest allows anyone to follow or comment unless restrictions are set.

2. Manage who can follow or contact your teen

- Go to Settings > Home feed tuner > People and boards.
- Remove unwanted followers or mute content from specific users.

3. To block a user:

- Visit their profile.
- Click the three-dot icon, then select Block.

Pinterest may suggest or display mature content unless filtered.

4. Limit exposure to sensitive content

- Go to Settings > Home feed tuner.

- Choose Boards, Pins, and Interests to remove or refine suggestions.
- Use the "I don't like this Pin" option to train recommendations in real time.

If your teen comes across harmful, graphic, or misleading content, they can report it directly.

5. Report inappropriate content or users

- Click the three-dot icon on the pin or user profile.
- Select Report Pin or Report User.
- Choose the reason and follow the steps.

Pinterest uses activity and profile data to serve targeted ads.

6. Disable or limit personalized ad tracking

- Go to Settings > Privacy and data.
- Toggle off Use sites you visit to improve which recommendations and ads you see.
- Toggle off 'Use info from our partners to improve recommendations and ads.'

Reddit

Reddit is one of the most popular social media platforms worldwide. It is known for its discussion-based forums (subreddits), memes, news, and viral content. While many adults use Reddit to stay informed, share interests, and participate in discussions, it is not always a safe space for children.

Reddit is mainly unmoderated and community-driven, meaning that kids can easily be exposed to explicit content, predators, dangerous trends, and scams if they aren't careful. Reddit hosts adult content that isn't always blocked by default, and some subreddits promote violence, bullying, and extremist views.

Privacy and safety settings:

Reddit profiles are public by default. That means anyone can see your teen's post history, comments, and community memberships.

1. Limit account visibility

- Go to Settings > Account settings > Profile.
- Turn off Show active communities you're in.
- Turn off Content visibility to prevent posts from appearing on the public profile.
- Encourage your teen to avoid using real names or personal details in their username or bio.

By default, Reddit allows strangers to send chat requests or private messages. Limiting this can reduce the chances of unwanted contact.

2. Restrict who can message or chat

- Go to Settings > Privacy & security > Chat and messaging settings.

- Set Who can send chat requests to Nobody or People you follow.
- Set Who can message you to Nobody or Trusted users only.

If your child is ever contacted by someone who makes them uncomfortable, they should know how to stop further contact immediately.

3. Block or report users who behave inappropriately

- Click the three-dot icon next to a post, comment, or username.
- Select Block user to stop all future interactions.
- Select Report to notify Reddit of inappropriate content or behavior.

Some Reddit communities share sensitive content, which can be mature or explicit. You can turn this off completely in your child's settings.

4. Filter out adult or sensitive content

- Go to Settings > Feed settings.
- Turn off sensitive content.
- Turn on Blur sensitive images in feed to hide any flagged images.
- Customize the Home feed by filtering out specific communities (subreddits) that aren't age-appropriate.

Reddit shows what your child has upvoted or downvoted, and it saves their comment and post history. Limiting what's visible on their profile adds a layer of privacy.

5. Hide voting and activity history

    - Go to Profile > Settings (gear icon).
    - Turn off Show upvotes and Show downvotes.

Twitch

Twitch is a live-streaming platform primarily used for watching and broadcasting gaming content. It also hosts streams related to music, art, podcasts, and "Just Chatting" sessions, where streamers talk directly with their audience. While it was originally geared toward gamers, Twitch has grown into a broader entertainment space that appeals to teens for its live, interactive format and community-driven feel.

Teens use Twitch to follow their favorite streamers, chat with other viewers, or even stream themselves. Unlike pre-recorded content on platforms like YouTube, Twitch streams happen in real time. This means the content is less filtered, and the chat moves quickly, sometimes faster than moderators can keep up.

Twitch offers both public and subscriber-based streams. Viewers can interact via live chat, send reactions, and tip streamers through donations or paid subscriptions. While many streamers maintain a friendly and welcoming space, some may feature mature language, adult humor, or heated discussions. Twitch does have age restrictions (users must be 13 or older), but there are no robust age verification tools in place.

Privacy and safety settings:

Twitch chat can move quickly and may contain offensive or inappropriate language. Enabling chat filters can help block harmful content before it appears.

1. Filter inappropriate chat messages

    - Go to Settings (gear icon) in any stream's chat window.

2. Choose Chat Filters.

    - Toggle on filters for Discrimination, Sexually Explicit Language, Hostility, and Profanity.

Whispers are Twitch's private messaging feature. Disabling them can reduce unsolicited messages from strangers.

3. Restrict or turn off private messages (Whispers)

    - Go to Settings > Security and Privacy.
    - Under Privacy, toggle off Block Whispers from strangers.
    - You can also block specific users by clicking their name > three-dot menu > Block.

While Twitch doesn't allow traditional friend requests, it's possible to limit interactions by adjusting follower and messaging settings.

4. Control who can follow or message your teen

    - Go to Settings > Security and Privacy.
    - Enable Phone or Email Verification under Channel

Moderation.

- Block or report abusive users as needed using the three-dot icon on their profile.

Not all streams are appropriate for teens. Streamers can mark their streams as "Mature," but this setting isn't enforced through age verification.

5. Limit access to mature content

- Use Twitch while logged into your teen's account.
- Avoid streams labeled Mature Content. Twitch will show a warning screen before these streams load.
- Discuss appropriate streamers and categories with your teen occasionally.

Twitch offers in-app purchases like Bits, Subscriptions, and Gifted Subs, which can add up quickly. Make sure to avoid linking payment methods directly to your child's account, and use Twitch Gift Cards for more controlled access to paid features.

6. Manage Twitch spending and subscriptions

- Go to Wallet > Payment History to monitor or disable active subscriptions.

If your child is planning to stream on Twitch, setting up moderation is essential for managing live chat.

7. Review moderation tools:

- Go to Creator Dashboard > Settings > Moderation.

- Enable AutoMod, which holds potentially harmful messages for review.
- Assign a trusted friend or adult as a Moderator to help manage the chat during streams.

Zigazoo

Zigazoo is a video-based social media app designed specifically for kids and younger teens. It encourages kids to record and upload videos and respond to various challenges or prompts. Unlike most platforms, Zigazoo is built around closed-loop engagement, meaning users respond to challenges and prompts by posting short videos and can only react with pre-approved emojis and responses.

However, children may unknowingly share personal details in their videos, such as their real name, school, or location, without realizing how dangerous that can be. Even though Zigazoo is moderated, videos can still be publicly viewable. This means that strangers can see what a child looks like, what they enjoy, and where they might be.

From a cybersecurity standpoint, Zigazoo stands out for what it removes rather than what it adds. There are no open comments, no direct messaging, and no public follower counts. All content is human-moderated before it's made visible to others. For children under 13, parental approval is required during sign-up, and controls are managed through a parent dashboard. These choices reduce common online risks such as grooming, bullying, and exposure to inappropriate content.

That said, Zigazoo isn't without its complexities. While it doesn't encourage the kind of virality seen on platforms like TikTok or Instagram, it still introduces children to social validation through Zigs (likes) and brand-sponsored challenges. The content is framed as educational and creative, but the gamified nature can still lead to performative behavior. The app also collects behavioral data, as most digital platforms do.

Privacy and safety settings:

Zigazoo limits public access, but parents can reinforce privacy by disabling public discoverability.

1. Set the account to private

   - Go to your child's profile settings from the parent account.
   - Turn off Appear in search results and toggle Private Profile ON.

All videos are moderated, but parents can also preview or delete content.

2. Review posted videos before they go public

   - Open your parent dashboard.
   - Navigate to My Child's Videos.
   - View, edit, or delete any submission before it becomes visible.

Many challenges are fun and educational, but some are branded or promotional.

3. Limit exposure to brand-sponsored or promotional challenges

- Browse challenges alongside your child.
- Encourage participation in educational or school-related prompts.
- Avoid challenges that include product placement or commercial themes.

While unsolicited contact is rare due to Zigazoo's design, users can still encounter content or behavior they'd prefer to avoid.

4. Block or report inappropriate behavior

- Navigate to the user's profile or their video.
- Tap the three-dot icon (⁝) near their video or username.
- Select Block User to prevent your child from seeing their content.
- Select Report to notify Zigazoo's moderation team.

Intermission

Thank you for reading *A Parent's Guide to Online Safety* so far. I hope you have found the information helpful and feel much more confident about keeping your children safe online. Before we move on to the next part of this book, I have a small favor to ask. Your feedback is precious to me and will help other parents discover this book. If you are enjoying reading it and finding the tips helpful, please write a review.

"He who said money can't buy happiness hasn't given enough away!"

<u>If you are on Audible,</u> hit the three dots at the top right of your device, click Rate and Review, and leave a few sentences about the book with a star rating.

<u>If you are reading on Kindle or an e-reader,</u> scroll to the bottom of the book, swipe up, and it will prompt a review.

If, for some reason, these changed - you can go to the Amazon review page here:
https://www.amazon.com/review/create-review/?ie=UTF8&channel=glance-detail&asin=1967793107

If you're reading the paperback, you can scan this QR code, which will take you directly to the Amazon reviews section.

Just scan the code with your phone's camera and click on the link that pops up. It is one of the few times it is OK to click on a link!

Thank you from the bottom of my heart. It is people like you who help to make the world a better place.

CHAPTER 5

Cyber Hygiene

Building a safe online environment

In this chapter, we'll talk about Cyber hygiene, a term that sounds technical but is as fundamental as teaching your child to wash their hands before meals. Cyber hygiene refers to the daily practices and precautions we take to maintain the health and security of our digital environments. It encompasses everything from the simple act of locking screens to prevent unauthorized access to educating children on recognizing secure websites marked by HTTPS.

Basics of cyber hygiene

Cyber hygiene is about small, consistent habits that build a strong foundation.

Think of it like maintaining a car: it needs regular checkups, not just repairs after something breaks. The same goes for your devices. Phones, laptops, smart TVs, and anything that connects to the internet needs regular software updates. These updates carry crucial security patches that close gaps hackers could otherwise exploit. Turning on automatic updates takes the burden off your memory and keeps you one step ahead without much effort.

Similarly, make sure you use an up-to-date antivirus and anti-malware software on your laptops and PCs. These programs work in the background, scanning for suspicious activity at the device level and alert you to potential dangers.

Password management is another cornerstone of cyber hygiene. Strong, unique passwords are essential, but we all know that remembering and maintaining unique passwords for each of our digital accounts is not easy. This is where password managers can help. These tools securely store your passwords, allowing you to create complex combinations without the fear of forgetting them. You can even use notebooks to physically write passwords down. This method may seem "old school," but consider this: they are impossible to hack from the outside world.

Backing up your data comes next. Regular data backups protect against loss from hardware failures or, more importantly, cyberattacks. Cloud storage solutions offer a convenient way to automate this process. For an additional layer of security, external hard drives provide a physical backup option that can be stored safely at home. But be sure to disconnect them and keep them in a safe place once the backup is completed.

Operating system-specific privacy settings are often overlooked but play a crucial role in maintaining your privacy online. These settings allow you to control what personal data is collected and shared by your devices. Take a few minutes now and then to review what's being collected. Better yet, walk your kids through the process.

Cyber hygiene checklist

Encourage your family to practice good cyber hygiene with this daily checklist. Use it as a guide to instill healthy digital habits:

- Lock screens when devices are not in use.
- Verify websites are secure (look for HTTPS in the URL or website address).
- Schedule automatic software updates for anything that connects to your network.
- Use a password manager or notebook for all accounts.
- Back up data weekly to cloud or external drives.
- Review privacy settings monthly.
- Set up 2FA for all accounts you create.

All of these habits are personal layers of protection. These habits may seem small, but together they form the backbone of a safer, more intentional life online. They secure your information and your digital life. At the next layer, we'll look into the network connecting everything in your home. From phones and laptops to smart TVs, doorbells, and speakers, your home Wi-Fi is the central hub. If it isn't properly secured, even the best device-level precautions can be bypassed.

Protecting Your Home Network

Let's now shift focus from individual devices to the broader ecosystem. Your router and modem are the gatekeepers of your family's internet connection, linking every smartphone, tablet, camera, or smart speakers (Alexa, Google Nest, etc.). Anything that connects to the internet, whether it's a child's iPad, your work laptop, or a smart TV, is passing through this same central pathway. If that pathway isn't secure, neither are the devices using it.

A typical home setup includes two main components:

- The modem, which connects you to your internet service provider.
- The router, which sends that connection wirelessly to your devices.

Sometimes these are bundled into one box. If you're not sure which one you have, it's worth checking, since these devices sit at the heart of everything your family does online.

Out of personal experience, I can tell you that many home networks are vulnerable by default. Routers often come with factory-set usernames and passwords which are the same across every unit of that model. Many families never change them. Some forget to set a password at all. And when software updates are ignored (routers need updates too!), known flaws go unpatched, leaving the door wide open.

One of the simplest and most important things you can do is change the default login credentials for your router. These are not the Wi-Fi name and password your kids use to connect their phones. This is the separate login used to access the router's settings, usually through a browser. The default username is often "admin," and the password might literally be "password" or a short string printed on the side of the device. This password, often included in the packaging, is widely known and easily exploited. Change both to something unique and strong.

Next, rename your Wi-Fi network to something that doesn't identify you or your household. Avoid using your family's last name or your street address in the network name (SSID). Something neutral like "BluePine_5G" is fine. Then set a strong Wi-Fi password, avoid pet names, birthdays, or favorite sports teams.

Next, ensure that your network uses WPA3 encryption. This protocol encrypts your data, making it unreadable for anyone who intercepts it. If your router doesn't support WPA3, consider upgrading to one that does.

Some routers also offer guest networks, which are great for keeping devices separate. You can create a separate network just for your child's devices, or for visiting friends. This limits what those devices can access on your main network and reduces the risk of accidental exposure to malware, as we saw in Matt's case.

And here's something many people miss: your router's admin interface, the settings page you access through your browser, should not be accessible from outside your home. If remote management is enabled, turn it off. Unless you specifically need to log in to your router from somewhere else, there's no reason to leave it open.

Regular updates to your router's firmware are essential in closing security gaps. Manufacturers frequently release updates to patch vulnerabilities, much like software updates for computers or smartphones. Setting your router to update automatically ensures it remains protected against the latest threats without requiring manual intervention.

It's also worth restarting your router periodically and checking for firmware updates from the manufacturer. Many newer models allow you to enable automatic updates, and if yours does, it's a good idea to turn that on. Just like your phone or laptop, your router needs updates to stay ahead of security vulnerabilities.

As a parent, it's natural to focus only on the content your child is seeing, but if that content travels through an unsafe and vulnerable network, cybercriminals can plant malicious software, reroute your traffic, or even monitor your family's browsing in real time.

What to Know When Kids Are Shopping Online

Online shopping is now a part of everyday life for kids and adults alike. What starts as browsing for game upgrades or a cool hoodie quickly turns into a rabbit hole of product recommendations, influencer promos, and limited-time deals.

Teens and children can now visit virtual shopping malls, where platforms like Steam, Xbox, PlayStation Store, Nintendo eShop, and Epic Games offer an array of digital products. In addition to selling online games, these platforms offer in-game items like skins, weapons, and downloadable content (DLCs).

While this virtual shopping experience is exciting, the risks are real. Unauthorized purchases become problematic when credit card details are linked to these accounts, often leading to surprise charges that frustrate parents. It's essential to maintain oversight, ensuring that spending limits are set and purchases are pre-approved to avoid unwelcome surprises.

Beyond gaming, platforms like Amazon, Etsy, AliExpress, and eBay offer a world of options: gadgets, toys, collectibles, and clothing that speak directly to a child's interests. While this access is exciting, it comes with trade-offs.

Not every seller on these platforms is trustworthy. Counterfeit products, fake listings, and vague return policies are more common than most first-time shoppers realize. Some sellers bank on the fact that kids and teens don't think to check the fine print. That's why your child needs to know how to recognize red flags:

- Poor or absent reviews
- Oddly low prices
- No clear return policy
- Sellers with no history

These might seem like small details, but they often separate a smooth purchase from a frustrating (and sometimes costly) lesson.

Social media adds another layer. TikTok Shop, Instagram ads, and Facebook Marketplace blur the line between entertainment and advertising. A product promoted by a favorite influencer feels trustworthy and even personal. But kids do not know that most of these are paid promotions done by people who have never actually used the said product. Many also partner with drop-shipping stores or sellers with little accountability once the money changes hands.

Fake stores and impulse buying can lead to unintended consequences, including privacy concerns and financial strain. If your child is shopping through social platforms, help them slow down.

- Look up the seller.

- Ask where the product is shipping from.
- Look for reviews that sound human and not like bots.

Then there are app stores, streaming services, and music platforms. Many of these apps offer free trials that automatically convert into paid subscriptions. If you're not actively tracking renewals, the charges pile up quietly. It's important to walk your child through how subscriptions work.

- Show the kids how to check which subscriptions are active.
- Guide them to periodically review active subscriptions and cancel those that are not needed anymore.
- Teach them how to spot when a "free" app isn't actually free in the long run.

When it comes to online shopping, the risks go beyond just spending too much. Purchases involve handing over personal details: names, addresses, emails, and saved payment methods. If that data lands in the wrong hands, the consequences can be far-reaching. Here are a few steps you can take to make online shopping safer for your child:

- Set up spending limits.
- Enable parental controls for in-app purchases.
- Talk about how to recognize scams and what to do when something doesn't feel right.
- Always stick with secure payment methods like credit cards that offer fraud protection.

- Make online shopping part of your family's conversations about money. Not just how much things cost, but what makes something worth buying.
- Teach them how to spot a deal and how to walk away from one that's too good to be true.

These early lessons in financial literacy and digital awareness are skills that your child would carry well into adulthood.

Using Parental Controls Without Overreach

Parental controls are invaluable in managing children's online activity. It safeguards young users while allowing them to explore, exactly what a parent would want. These controls help limit screen time and restrict access to age-appropriate content.

Most smartphones and tablets have built-in controls, such as Screen Time on iOS, allowing you to set app usage limits and manage downtime. On gaming consoles and smart TVs, features exist to restrict access to mature games and content. Configuring these settings can be as simple as navigating to the device's settings menu, selecting the parental controls option, and following the prompts to customize the restrictions to fit your family's needs.

However, the key to adequate parental controls lies in striking a balance between protection and privacy. Rather than acting as a digital surveillance system, these controls should serve as a gentle guideline. It's important to remember that parental controls are most effective when used as part of a broader strategy that includes open communication.

- Encourage conversations about online boundaries.

- Explain why certain restrictions exist and how they contribute to safety.
- Address any privacy concerns your child may have.
- Ensure they understand that the goal is not to invade their space but to protect them from potential dangers.

Open communication about monitoring practices helps build trust in kids and reinforces that these measures are in place for their benefit. Setting mutual agreements and digital contracts with your children can further solidify this understanding. By involving them in decision-making, you empower them to take ownership of their online behaviors and foster a sense of responsibility.

Several tools and resources can assist in maintaining adequate parental controls for ongoing management. Apps like Google Family Link and Microsoft Family Safety offer comprehensive features that extend beyond simple restrictions. These tools help parents stay informed and responsive to their children's evolving digital habits.

CHAPTER 6

Your Child's Digital Footprint

How to understand and manage it?

When you do anything online, you leave an indelible trace, whether through social media interactions, browsing history, or shared content. Unlike paper records that can be discarded or shredded, a digital footprint lasts *forever*. The information accumulated online can shape a child's future reputation, influence opportunities, and even present potential risks to their safety and privacy.

Given the permanence of digital footprints, parents must understand how to guide their children in managing their online presence responsibly. A proactive approach ensures that children know the long-term consequences of their digital actions while equipping them with the tools necessary to safeguard personal information.

What Is a Digital Footprint?

A digital footprint is generally categorized into two distinct types: active and passive.

An active digital footprint refers to any information intentionally shared by a child. This includes social media posts, online comments, uploaded videos, and other consciously published content.

Conversely, a passive digital footprint consists of data collected without direct user involvement. Websites and applications track user behavior, record browsing history, and monitor interactions through cookies and location services. While an active footprint is typically within the user's control, a passive footprint often requires deliberate actions to minimize exposure.

Why it matters?

Every time your child posts a photo, creates a username, joins an app, or even clicks on a link, it is being recorded somewhere by someone. Whether your child is 8 or 18, they're already building this ongoing trail of data. The question isn't *if* it matters—it's *how much* it matters, and whether they understand what they're leaving behind.

First, it affects privacy. Kids assume that when they delete a post, it's gone. But screenshots can be taken and old accounts can be archived. Deleted doesn't always mean erased. Digital footprints can stick around longer than we are aware of, sometimes years longer. What's shared impulsively at 13 might still exist when they're applying for college or internships.

Then there's the profiling. Companies use digital footprints to build detailed models of who your child is, what they like, what they might buy, and how they behave online. This influences everything from the ads the kids see to the type of content algorithms push their way. While this might seem like "harmless personalization" to the untrained eye, it shapes the online environment that the kids spend years in.

And perhaps most importantly, a digital footprint can affect your child's reputation. Inappropriate or poorly considered online interactions can resurface years later, affecting a child's academic or professional opportunities. College admissions officers and potential employers frequently review applicants' online presence, assessing their judgment and character based on past posts and public interactions. A single impulsive post, comment, or shared image may be taken out of context and used against them.

Oversharing has become an all-too-common phenomenon, where individuals disclose more personal information than necessary. Sharing a birthday post or a check-in at a favorite coffee shop might seem harmless, but these seemingly innocent actions can open doors to risks. For instance, a cybercriminal might use a birthdate combined with other public information about the victim to answer security questions and gain access to sensitive accounts. This type of information can also be used in social engineering attacks, where the perpetrator manipulates the victim into revealing even more data.

Take the scenario where teenagers frequently share their location through social media posts. This habit can inadvertently provide a detailed map of their daily routine, making it easier for someone with ill intentions to predict their whereabouts. In another instance, oversharing financial achievements or purchases can attract scammers who tailor their schemes to exploit perceived wealth or successes. Children who overshare personal information or express controversial opinions may become targets of digital aggression. Furthermore, ill-intentioned individuals could manipulate, doctor, or misrepresent their online activities.

That's not to say a child should never post or express themselves. But they need to understand the difference between something meant for close friends and something that can be found by anyone with a search bar.

Manage and Protect Your Child's Digital Footprint

Teaching kids to manage their digital presence starts with one core habit: *pausing before you post*. Encourage your child to think through the possible impact of what they're sharing. A helpful rule is the *billboard rule*: if they wouldn't be comfortable with a post being displayed publicly in front of their school, it's probably best not to post it.

Beyond what they share, it's just as important to help them understand how their information is shared behind the scenes. Walk them through how to set social media profiles to private, turn off location sharing, review app permissions, and limit contact from unknown users. These settings often exist but aren't always obvious, and this is where your guidance matters.

Managing a digital footprint also includes cleaning up what already exists. Sit down with your children once or twice a year to look themselves up online and go through past accounts. From there, they can remove unused profiles, adjust privacy settings, and delete anything outdated or unnecessary.

Here are a few strategies to follow to effectively manage a digital footprint:

- Avoid sharing full names, phone numbers, addresses, or school details in public posts or chats.
- Be cautious of unknown users who ask personal questions or offer free gifts.
- Recognize suspicious links or phishing attempts in emails, DMs, or comment sections.
- Ask for help if you ever feel unsure, uncomfortable, or pressured online.

These conversations don't need to be technical. They just need to be regular and honest. The goal isn't to scare your child but to give them tools and awareness so they can move through the internet with a little more caution and a lot more confidence.

Facial recognition and biometric data risks

Many kids today engage with the internet not just through words or clicks, but through their bodies, faces in selfies, voices in videos, even movement patterns in fitness apps or games. All of that falls under the umbrella of biometric data, and it's fast becoming one of the most sensitive forms of personal information your child may be sharing without knowing.

Biometric data includes physical characteristics like facial geometry, voice patterns, fingerprints, eye movement, and even how someone walks (also known as gait). This data is increasingly collected by apps and platforms that look harmless on the surface.

The issue is not just that this data is being used. It's how it's stored, shared, and monetized. Unlike a password, biometric data can't be changed if it's leaked or stolen. If a photo of your child's face is captured, analyzed, and stored on a third-party server, you have no way of knowing where that data might end up or how it might be used, now or ten years from now. Some platforms claim to anonymize data, but anonymized biometric data can often be re-identified when combined with other information.

For children, this exposure carries long-term consequences. Biometric data could be used for surveillance, targeted advertising, or in extreme cases, identity fraud. Facial recognition systems already exist in school security systems, smart home devices, and government databases. If your child's data ends up in the wrong dataset, it could follow them into adulthood.

Unfortunately, platforms don't always make it easy to opt out of biometric tracking. But there are ways to reduce exposure:

- Avoid uploading close-up face photos or videos on public settings, especially on platforms known for filters or face effects.

- Turn off "Face ID" features in apps and devices that don't absolutely require them. A passcode works just fine for most devices.

- Check app permissions regularly. Disable camera, microphone, and location access for apps that don't need them.

- In Snapchat, turn off "Lens data usage" by going to Settings > Additional Services > Manage > Permissions.

- In Instagram and TikTok, avoid AR filters that map facial expressions. These often require additional data access behind the scenes.

- Use browsers or operating systems that block cross-site tracking and fingerprinting, such as Safari's Intelligent Tracking Prevention or Firefox's Enhanced Tracking Protection.

Most importantly, talk to your child about what's happening behind the camera. Let them know that a fun face filter isn't just changing how they look, it's analyzing their features. Help them ask: *What does this app really need to see?* and *What am I giving it in return?*

Biometric data is personal in the most literal way. Once it's out there, you can't get it back. Teaching your child to think before sharing their face, voice, or behavior online is one of the most powerful habits they can learn. It's not about fear, it's about awareness, and protecting what makes them uniquely themselves.

Leveraging a digital footprint for positive impact

Although a digital footprint can present risks, it also offers opportunities for personal growth and career advancement. Encouraging children to curate a positive online presence can enhance their academic and professional prospects. For example, maintaining a blog, showcasing creative projects, or contributing to educational discussions can demonstrate valuable skills and interests.

Participation in online learning platforms, coding projects, or volunteering initiatives can add credibility to their digital presence. Moreover, using social media to engage in meaningful conversations or network with professionals can position children favorably.

CHAPTER 7

Hidden Dangers of Public Wi-Fi

The convenience and the cost

Public Wi-Fi is everywhere. From coffee shops and airports to libraries, restaurants, and even in schools, free internet access is now seen as a basic service. It allows people to stay connected without using mobile data, making it an appealing option for children and teens who are constantly online. Free Wi-Fi can be a lifesaver for users with limited data plans. It's a convenient way to stay online without eating through mobile data. And with many families managing limited data plans, public Wi-Fi often feels like a helpful solution.

However, public Wi-Fi networks often lack proper security, making them prime targets for cybercriminals looking to steal personal information. They are unsecured, meaning the data moving through them isn't encrypted or protected. If your child logs into social media, sends messages, or uses apps while connected to an open network, their personal information could be quietly intercepted.

This chapter will explain the most significant threats that accompany a public Wi-Fi connection. Understanding how these networks work and why they can be dangerous is essential. When your child knows what to look out for, they're far more likely to make safer choices about when and where to connect.

Man-in-the-Middle (MitM) attacks

A Man-in-the-Middle (MitM) attack occurs when a hacker intercepts the communication between a user's device and a Wi-Fi network. This allows the hacker to monitor, alter, or steal sensitive data secretly. Public Wi-Fi networks, especially those without encryption, are prime targets for this attack.

Here's how an MitM attack works:

Interception: The hacker positions themselves between a user's phone, tablet, or laptop and the public Wi-Fi router. This can be done using special software or by setting up a rogue access point mimicking a legitimate Wi-Fi network.

Eavesdropping: Once connected, the attacker monitors the victim's internet traffic. This means they can see unencrypted login credentials, emails, messages, and even financial transactions if they are not properly encrypted.

Data theft or manipulation: The attacker captures sensitive information or modifies data in real-time. For example, if your child logs into their school account, the hacker could intercept their username and password, gaining unauthorized access.

Fake Wi-Fi networks (Evil Twin attacks)

An Evil Twin attack is a cyberattack where hackers create a fraudulent Wi-Fi network that appears to be a legitimate public hotspot. The goal is to trick users into connecting, allowing the attacker to steal personal information, monitor online activity, and inject malware onto the victim's device.

Here's how an Evil Twin attack works:

Creating a fake network: Hackers set up a Wi-Fi network with a name (SSID) that mimics a trusted public network. This could be something like:

- "Starbucks_Guest" (instead of the actual "StarbucksWiFi")
- "Library_FreeWiFi" (instead of the actual "CityLibrary_WiFi")
- "Airport_Hotspot" (instead of the actual "JFK_Airport_WiFi")

Tricking users into connecting: Most people don't double-check a public Wi-Fi network's exact name before connecting, especially in a rush. If your child clicks on the wrong Wi-Fi name, they might unknowingly connect to the hacker's hotspot instead of the real one.

Intercepting data: Once connected, the hacker can monitor all online activity in real-time, including:

- Login credentials for social media, email, and banking apps

- Private messages sent over chat apps
- Browsing history and website visits
- Credit card details, if entered on an unsecured website

Injecting malware or phishing attacks: In some cases, hackers go beyond spying and actively manipulate what victims see on their devices. For example:

Fake pop-ups that request a user to "re-enter" their password, which the hacker then steals.

Automatic malware downloads, infecting the victim's phone or computer with spyware or ransomware.

Data sniffing and eavesdropping

Many public Wi-Fi networks lack encryption, meaning data is transmitted in plain, understandable format. This makes it easy for hackers to "listen in" to the information sent and received.

In data sniffing attacks, cybercriminals intercept internet traffic in real time to steal sensitive information such as usernames, passwords, messages, and browsing history.

Here's how data sniffing works:

Using packet sniffers: Hackers use special software known as packet sniffers (such as Wireshark) to capture data packets traveling between devices and the Wi-Fi router. This allows them to see:

- Logins to social media, email, and banking accounts

- Messages sent over unencrypted chat apps
- Websites visited and forms filled out

Decryption of sensitive data: While some websites and apps use encryption, hackers can sometimes force victims to visit a site's unencrypted (HTTP) version. This technique, known as SSL stripping, removes the security layer, exposing usernames, passwords, and other personal details.

Malware injection

Cybercriminals can distribute malware by compromising public Wi-Fi networks, especially those that are poorly maintained. Simply connecting to a network, downloading a file, or visiting an infected website can put your family's personal data and the entire device at risk.

Here's how malware injection works:

Infected Wi-Fi networks: Hackers compromise a public Wi-Fi network (such as one in a café, school, or shopping mall) and inject malware into connected devices without the users' knowledge.

Drive-by downloads: Your child may unknowingly download malware by visiting an infected website or clicking on a legitimate-looking pop-up. These downloads happen in the background, and malicious software is installed without warning.

Fake software updates and apps: Cybercriminals create fake software update prompts that appear when someone is connected to the infected network. If your child sees a pop-up that says, *"Your device needs an urgent security update,"* they might click it, unknowingly installing spyware, adware, or ransomware.

Man-in-the-Browser attacks: In some cases, malware injected via public Wi-Fi can alter what your child sees on their browser. This can lead to:

- Fake login pages that steal passwords.
- Redirects to phishing websites that mimic popular platforms.
- Forcing pop-ups that trick users into downloading more malware.

True story: Scammed at the mall

A routine shopping trip became a nightmare for 12-year-old Lena.

Lena and her friend Mia were at the mall after school, grabbing snacks and browsing stores when Lena noticed her phone's data signal was weak. She spotted a free Wi-Fi network with the mall's name and connected without thinking twice. It looked legitimate; no password required, full signal strength, and the word *"official"* was present in the network's name.

Minutes later, Mia received a DM on her Instagram from Lena saying she had won a $50 gift card. Mia knew that Lena couldn't have sent this message because she was right there talking to her.

What Lena discovered only much later was that the Wi-Fi network was a trap. The hacker who set up the network intercepted her online activity, and within minutes, he had locked her out of her email and Instagram accounts.

Panicked by the discovery, Lena and Mia went straight to the mall's customer service desk. Security staff contacted Lena's mother, who arrived shortly after. She acted fast, freezing the bank account, resetting passwords, and calling their bank's fraud department. Mall IT staff checked the Wi-Fi and confirmed that the network Lena had joined wasn't one of theirs.

Despite the quick response, Lena's Instagram account couldn't be recovered. She had to start over. And while no money was lost, the family was warned that the stolen credentials may end up for sale on the dark web, exposing them to future fraud.

"This wasn't just about losing an Instagram account. It could have cost us money or worse," said Lena's mother. "We never thought a simple mall trip could turn into a security breach."

Authorities are investigating the attack, but cybercriminals using fake Wi-Fi networks often remain anonymous, leaving victims with few options for justice. Experts warn that public Wi-Fi scams are becoming increasingly common in malls, airports, and coffee shops. Always verify official Wi-Fi networks with staff before connecting, avoid entering passwords or banking information on public networks, and use cellular data or a VPN for sensitive activities.

"I thought I was just saving data," Lena remarked. "Now I know how easy it is for things to go wrong. I won't make that mistake again."

How to Keep Your Child Safe on Public Wi-Fi?

While the best practice is to avoid public Wi-Fi whenever possible, it isn't always possible. So, here's how you can minimize the risks if you need to connect to a public Wi-Fi network:

1. **Turn off Auto-Connect:** Devices often automatically connect to familiar networks, which can be dangerous if

a hacker sets up a fake Wi-Fi hotspot with the same name as a trusted location.

- On iPhone: Settings > Wi-Fi > Auto-Join Hotspots > Ask to Join
- On Android: Settings > Wi-Fi > Turn off Auto Connect

2. **Verify the network name:** Before connecting to public Wi-Fi, teach your child to ask a staff member for the correct network name. Hackers often set up fake networks with slightly different names.

3. **Use mobile data instead of Wi-Fi:** Encourage your child to use their mobile data instead of public Wi-Fi, especially when logging into accounts or making purchases. If they don't have unlimited data, consider setting up a hotspot from your phone.

4. **Disable file sharing and Bluetooth:** Hackers can exploit file-sharing settings to send malware or access stored files. Teach your child to turn off Bluetooth and AirDrop unless they're actively using it.

   - On Windows: Control Panel > Network and Sharing Center > Advanced Sharing Settings > Turn off File Sharing.
   - On Mac: System Preferences > Sharing > Uncheck File Sharing
   - On iPhone: Settings > General > AirDrop > Receiving Off

- On Android: Settings > Bluetooth > Off

5. **Log out of accounts when finished:** If your child must use public Wi-Fi, log out of accounts afterward and clear saved login credentials to prevent stored session cookies from being hijacked.

6. **Enable Two-Factor Authentication (2FA):** Even if a hacker steals a password, 2FA can block them from logging in. Enable two-factor authentication on all critical accounts, especially email, social media, and banking apps.

Public Wi-Fi is convenient, but it comes with serious risks. Encourage your child to think of public Wi-Fi like a public park, it's OK to use it, but you wouldn't want to share personal secrets with strangers. Staying alert and practicing smart online habits are the best ways to stay safe on a public Wi-Fi.

CHAPTER 8

Malware and Viruses

Types of malware parents should know

The basic definition of malware is that it is a software designed to steal information, damage files, spy on activities, and even take control of devices. But to effectively protect your family from cyberattacks, a deeper understanding of malware types and how each one operates is needed. This helps parents put the right protections in place. It's not just about installing antivirus software. If you know what spyware does, for example, you're more likely to check app permissions and keep an eye on what's running in the background. If you know what ransomware can do, you'll see why backing up files and teaching your kid not to click random links actually matters.

The Different Types

Children often unknowingly expose themselves and their families to malware simply by clicking on an innocent-looking ad, downloading a game from an untrustworthy site, or opening an email attachment from an unknown sender. Once a single device on a network is infected, the malware can spread to other devices on the same network, putting family privacy at risk.

Here are the common types of malware that you need to know of to stay a step ahead in ensuring your family's cybersecurity.

Viruses

Viruses are the most common type of malware. A virus is a malicious program that attaches to legitimate files or software and spreads to other files or devices when the infected file is executed. Once activated, a virus can corrupt data, slow system performance, turn off essential programs, or render a device entirely unusable.

One infamous example is the *ILOVEYOU* virus, which spread rapidly in the early 2000s. The virus disguised itself as a text file, and when opened, overwrote critical files, corrupted system functions, and spread to contacts through email. While the *ILOVEYOU* virus primarily infected through email attachments, modern viruses often use torrent sites and unauthorized downloads as distribution methods, hiding within game installers, software cracks, and media files.

Another well-known virus is the *CIH* or *Chernobyl* virus, which was particularly destructive. It targeted system files and rendered computers unbootable. This type of malware often lurks within downloads, waiting for an unsuspecting user to open the infected file.

The *Melissa* virus spread via Microsoft Word documents, using macros to execute malicious commands once a document was opened. This proves that even non-executable files can be carriers of dangerous code.

Viruses continue to evolve. They are becoming highly sophisticated and better concealed with each day. They often manage to go unnoticed until significant damage has been done, emphasizing the importance of downloading software only from reputable sources and maintaining updated antivirus software.

Trojans

Trojans are among the most deceptive types of malware. Named after the infamous wooden horse of Greek mythology, trojans disguise themselves as legitimate software or files, tricking users into willingly downloading and executing them. Unlike viruses, which replicate themselves, trojans rely on social engineering tactics to access a device where they can carry out various malicious activities.

One of the most notorious trojans in history is the *Zeus*, which targeted banking credentials by capturing keystrokes and hijacking login sessions. *Zeus* spread through downloads and email attachments, compromising millions of devices worldwide. Similarly, the *Emotet* has been widely used to install other types of malware, making infected devices vulnerable to ransomware, financial fraud, and data theft.

Trojans often come bundled with cracked games, pirated software, or fake system updates. Gaming-related trojans, such as the *Steam Stealer*, are designed to steal login credentials for popular online gaming platforms, allowing hackers to access and sell valuable in-game items. Others, such as the *FakeAV*, impersonate antivirus software, tricking users into installing what appears to be a security tool but is designed to disable real security programs and open the door for further infections.

The effects of trojans can range from mild annoyances, such as system slowdowns and unwanted pop-ups, to severe consequences, including remote device control, theft of sensitive information, and complete data loss. Some trojans even install additional malware without the user's knowledge, leading to an escalating cycle of infections that compromise individual devices and an entire home network.

Because trojans are designed to trick users into installing them, education is the best defense. Teaching children to be skeptical of free downloads, unknown links, and unsolicited software updates can help them avoid becoming victims of these highly deceptive cyber threats.

Ransomware

Ransomware is the most destructive form of malware. It locks files and demands a ransom to unlock them, often in cryptocurrency. Once ransomware takes over, there's usually no way to recover files unless you've backed them up.

One of the most infamous ransomware attacks in history was *WannaCry*, which spread globally in 2017, infecting hundreds of thousands of computers. It exploited vulnerabilities in outdated operating systems, locking users out of their data and demanding payment in cryptocurrency. Another example is *Ryuk*, which targeted businesses and individuals alike, encrypting critical files and demanding large sums for decryption keys.

Ransomware infiltrates a system through downloads. For example, a child looking for a free version of a popular game may unknowingly install ransomware disguised as a game installer. Once executed, the malware encrypts files and displays a ransom note demanding payment to unlock them. Some variants go even further, threatening to publish stolen personal information online if the victim refuses to pay.

Beyond the financial burden, ransomware attacks are personally devastating. Families lose irreplaceable photos, documents, and other important files. Additionally, attackers use countdown timers to pressure victims into quick decisions.

Prevention is the best defense against ransomware. Regularly updating operating systems and using anti-ransomware software can help protect against vulnerabilities exploited by ransomware attacks. Teaching children the dangers of downloading software from unverified sources and encouraging them to use legitimate platforms can significantly reduce the risk of infection.

Spyware

Unlike other types of malware that cause immediate disruption, spyware operates discreetly in the background. This makes it one of the most dangerous threats. It records keystrokes, captures screenshots, tracks browsing activity, and even accesses a device's microphone or camera. Spyware can activate built-in webcams and microphones without the user's knowledge. Once activated, these compromised devices can secretly record audio and video, capturing private conversations, personal moments, and financial details. This breach of security can be particularly concerning for families with children, as predators and cybercriminals exploit stolen recordings for extortion or other malicious purposes.

One of the most famous examples of spyware is *FinFisher*, which tracks online communications and extracts data from infected devices.

Children and teenagers are particularly vulnerable to spyware because they often download apps and games from unofficial sources. Some spyware is disguised as parental control software, tricking users into installing it by claiming it will enhance security or device performance. Once installed, spyware can log everything the child types, including passwords, private messages, and credit card information, putting the child and their family at risk.

Safe browsing habits and security software are the best defenses against spyware. Teaching children to download only from official app stores, avoiding clicking on suspicious links, and never granting unnecessary app permissions can help prevent spyware infections. Additionally, install reputable antivirus software and run regular security scans to detect and remove spyware before it causes harm.

Worms

Worms spread independently across networks, infecting multiple devices without user interaction. Unlike viruses, which require a host file to execute and replicate, worms are self-replicating and can spread through vulnerabilities in operating systems, email attachments, or even instant messaging applications.

Blaster Worm, from the early 2000s, exploited a security flaw in Windows systems, allowing it to spread from one machine to another without user interaction. Once infected, computers crashed or restarted unexpectedly, disrupting businesses, institutions, and home users.

Another example is the *Conficker*, which infected millions of machines worldwide and created backdoors for hackers to gain control over infected devices, potentially leading to massive botnet attacks.

Because worms can spread without user interaction, they are challenging to contain. Keeping operating systems and security software up to date is essential to preventing worm infections. Also educate children on the risks of downloading from unverified sources, as worms typically disguise themselves as legitimate software.

Adware

Adware is designed to bombard users with excessive advertisements, often pop-ups, banners, and redirects. While adware is not always outright destructive, like ransomware or trojans, it significantly degrades a device's performance, compromises user privacy, and exposes children to inappropriate or fraudulent content.

Adware typically finds its way onto devices through free software downloads. Many of these "free" programs come with hidden adware that runs in the background, generating revenue for the developers by forcing users to view advertisements. Once installed, the adware can hijack web browsers, alter search results, redirect users to scam websites, and track browsing activity to deliver targeted ads. Some aggressive adware programs even install additional unwanted software without the user's knowledge, further clogging system resources and making devices sluggish and unresponsive.

One well-known example of adware is *Fireball*, which turned web browsers into advertising tools. *Fireball* manipulated search engine results to generate ad revenue and installed further malware, putting users at risk of more severe cyber threats.

Another widespread adware infection was *Gator*, which disguised itself as a helpful internet tool while secretly displaying intrusive ads and tracking user activity.

For children and teens, adware can be especially dangerous because the ads it generates lead to harmful content, including phishing websites, scam offers, or adult material. Some adware masquerade as fake virus alerts, tricking users into downloading more malware under the guise of security software. These scare tactics can lead to further infections.

While adware is often considered more of an annoyance than a severe cybersecurity threat, its potential to expose children to harmful content, degrade device performance, and open the door to additional malware infections makes it a risk worth addressing. Ensuring that devices have strong security settings can help minimize the risk of adware infections.

Virus Scanners and Firewalls

The best way to protect your family from malware is to implement security measures and teach your child safe browsing habits.

Antivirus

Installing a reliable antivirus program is one of the most effective ways to protect your family's devices from malware, viruses, and online threats. While purchasing and installing antivirus software might seem technical, it is a straightforward process that even non-technical parents can manage.

Many trusted antivirus providers are available, and purchasing a subscription can be done quickly online or in retail stores. Here are five reputable antivirus programs that provide excellent protection:

- **Norton 360:** One of the most well-known antivirus programs. Offers protection against malware, phishing, and online scams. Available on the Norton website or at major retailers like Best Buy and Amazon.

- **McAfee Total Protection:** Includes antivirus, firewall protection, and parental controls. Available on the McAfee website, as well as in electronics stores and online marketplaces.

- **Bitdefender Total Security:** A highly rated antivirus program with excellent malware detection rates. Can be purchased directly from the Bitdefender website or through online retailers.

- **Kaspersky Internet Security:** A well-regarded security program offering strong protection against ransomware and phishing. It can be found on the Kaspersky website and in physical stores.

- **Avast Premium Security:** A user-friendly antivirus program with protection against common cyber threats. Available on the Avast website and through various online retailers.

Once you've chosen and purchased an antivirus program, the installation process is simple and requires just a few steps:

Visit the official antivirus provider website and log in to your account. If you purchased a physical copy, follow the instructions to download the software.

Locate the downloaded file (usually in your computer's "Downloads" folder) and double-click it to begin the installation.

The installation wizard will guide you through the process. You may be asked to enter an activation key (provided at the time of purchase) to verify your subscription.

Once the installation is complete, restart your computer if prompted. The antivirus software should automatically activate and begin protecting your system.

Installing antivirus software is only one half of the process. Keeping it up to date is the other half. Most antivirus programs update automatically, but checking periodically is a good idea to ensure everything is running smoothly.

Firewalls

A firewall is a security feature that acts as a barrier between your device and potential threats from the internet. It monitors incoming and outgoing traffic and blocks unauthorized access, helping prevent cybercriminals from infiltrating your home network.

Most modern devices and routers have built-in firewalls that provide a basic level of security. Windows and macOS computers, for example, include pre-installed firewalls that can be enabled in the system settings. Additionally, many home routers have firewall protection enabled by default, adding another layer of defense at the network level.

Third-party firewall programs that provide advanced protection features are available for enhanced security. Some well-known firewall solutions include:

- **Norton Firewall:** This firewall is included in Norton 360 and helps prevent unauthorized access to your system.
- **Bitdefender Firewall:** Comes with Bitdefender Total Security and provides strong intrusion prevention features.
- **McAfee Firewall:** Part of McAfee Total Protection, this firewall monitors incoming and outgoing traffic for suspicious activity.
- **GlassWire:** A standalone firewall that provides real-time network monitoring and alerts users about unusual connections.
- **ZoneAlarm Firewall:** A widely used third-party firewall offering strong security features for home and business users.

Like antivirus software, firewalls receive updates to improve security. Ensure that automatic updates are enabled. If your firewall notifies you about suspicious activity, review the details to determine if action is needed.

CHAPTER 9

Password Management

Your first line of defense

Passwords are the first line of defense against cyber threats. But young internet users often make the mistake of using weak passwords that are easy to guess. Many also use the same password for several of their online accounts. That way, if a hacker gains access to one account, it often leads to full identity compromise (credential stuffing).

Picking strong passwords

Hackers commonly use brute-force attacks to crack passwords, where automated programs try thousands or even millions of password combinations until they find the correct one. This is why short, common passwords like "admin" or "password123" are especially dangerous.

A strong password should be unique and composed of a mix of uppercase and lowercase letters, numbers, and special characters. A strong passphrase or randomly generated password makes brute-force attacks nearly impossible, as the number of potential combinations becomes too large for even the most advanced hacking tools to crack.

However, remembering dozens of complicated passwords can be overwhelming, so consider using a password manager instead. Children and teenagers often have multiple accounts for school, gaming, and social media, making it challenging to track passwords without reusing them. With a password manager, they only need to remember one strong master password to access all their accounts securely.

Popular password managers like 1Password, LastPass, Bitwarden, and Dashlane work across multiple devices, phones, tablets, and laptops. They automatically sync your logins so your family can safely access what they need, when they need it. Many offer features like:

- Secure password sharing (so you can safely share streaming account logins with your teen safely)
- Alerts for breached or weak passwords
- Built-in two-factor authentication support
- Encrypted storage for sensitive notes like Wi-Fi passwords or school logins

Even better, most password managers offer family plans that allow you to protect multiple users under one account, perfect for households with teens or aging parents.

Enabling 2FA

Two-factor authentication (2FA) is another essential security measure that significantly enhances password protection. Even the strongest passwords can be stolen through phishing attacks, data breaches, or malware. That's why 2FA is crucial to protect your online accounts.

2FA requires users to provide two verification forms before logging into an account. The first factor is the password, and the second factor is usually something the user has (such as a mobile device, security key, or authentication app) or something the user *is* (such as a fingerprint or facial recognition).

Without 2FA, an attacker who has stolen or guessed a password can log in to an account without additional resistance. With 2FA, logging in requires both the password and the second authentication factor. Even if a hacker manages to steal a password, they still need the second layer of verification to log in. Many online platforms, including email providers, social media networks, and gaming accounts, offer 2FA as an option. Encourage your family to enable 2FA on all accounts where it is available.

Authentication apps, such as Google Authenticator, Microsoft Authenticator, and Authy, generate time-sensitive, one-time codes for the second authentication step. Unlike SMS, these codes are generated locally on the device and do not rely on a mobile network, making them immune to SIM-swapping attacks. These apps work even when the device is offline, providing a more secure and reliable method for two-factor authentication.

While young users may view 2FA as an inconvenience, they need to realize that the extra step is a small price to pay for significantly better security.

One more big threat to password security is social engineering, where cybercriminals manipulate victims into willingly giving up their passwords. Some attackers pose as customer service representatives or friends, convincing users to share login credentials. Teaching children never to share their passwords with anyone, not even friends, is essential to prevent social engineering attacks. With websites like *Have I Been Pwned* you can also periodically check if any of your credentials have ever been compromised during a data breach.

CHAPTER 10

Addressing Sensitive Topics

Children and teenagers are exposed to mature content earlier than ever, often before they fully understand its implications. Sexting and online pornography are no longer distant, adult-only topics. They are now easily accessible and, in many cases, actively marketed toward young audiences through social media, search engines, and peer interactions.

Many parents struggle with approaching these conversations, unsure when or how to begin. However, avoiding the discussion does not prevent exposure; instead, it increases the likelihood that children will seek answers elsewhere, often from unreliable sources. As uncomfortable as it may be, having an open, judgment-free dialogue about these issues is essential for equipping children with the knowledge and critical thinking skills needed to navigate the internet safely.

Sexting

Talking to your child about sexting can feel overwhelming, but avoiding the conversation doesn't prevent the risks. Sexting, which refers to the sharing of sexually explicit messages, images, or videos, has become a common issue among teenagers. Many young people don't fully understand the consequences, believing that messages disappear after they are deleted or that they can trust the person on the receiving end. As a parent, your role is to provide guidance, educate your children on the risks, and ensure they feel comfortable coming to you if they ever find themselves in a difficult situation.

Before you start the conversation, it's essential to understand why teenagers engage in sexting in the first place. Some see it as a way to express their emotions in a romantic relationship, while others feel pressured by a partner or peer. Some simply are curious, influenced by social media or the hypersexualized digital culture they are constantly exposed to. For some, it is an attempt to seek validation, believing that sending an image will gain them attention or approval. Some fall victim to manipulation, where an online predator or even a classmate convinces them that sharing explicit content is harmless or expected. Understanding these motivations helps you approach the conversation with empathy instead of judgment.

When bringing up the topic, choose a calm, judgment-free moment rather than waiting until you suspect an issue. A casual setting, such as during a car ride or while doing an activity together, can make the discussion less intimidating.

Start by asking open-ended questions rather than lecturing.

You might say, "I'm hearing so much about sexting in the news. Have you or your friends ever talked about it?" This allows them to share their thoughts and opinions before you provide guidance.

Explain sexting in a way that is appropriate for their age.

If they are younger, focus on the idea that sharing personal photos online can be dangerous because once something is sent, it's out of their control. A more detailed discussion about peer pressure, emotional consequences, and legal risks is necessary for older children. Make it clear that sexting is never just a private exchange between two people. Once an image is sent, it can be saved or even shared with others. Many teens falsely believe that apps like Snapchat, which claim to make messages disappear, are safe for this type of behavior. However, nothing truly disappears online. Screenshots can be taken, and even deleted files can sometimes be recovered.

Talk to your child about setting boundaries and recognizing red flags.

One of the most challenging aspects of sexting is peer pressure and coercion. Many young people are pressured into sending explicit photos, either because they believe it will make someone like them more or because they are afraid of losing a relationship. Let your child know that anyone who respects them will not pressure them to send such pictures. Reinforce the idea that saying no is not a sign of weakness, it is a sign of strength and self-respect.

Discuss the long-term consequences of sexting.

Many teenagers do not consider the emotional, reputational, and legal risks involved. Sharing an image beyond its intended recipient can lead to humiliation, bullying, and even blackmail. Victims of sexting-related leaks often suffer from anxiety, depression, and social isolation. Some have had to switch schools or delete their social media to escape harassment.

Beyond social consequences, there are also legal implications. In many places, possessing or distributing sexually explicit images of a minor, even if the minor took the image themselves, can be classified as child pornography, resulting in serious criminal charges. These are extreme consequences, but they happen, and your child needs to be aware of the risks.

While educating your child about these dangers is necessary, the conversation should not be rooted in fear alone. The goal is to empower them with knowledge so they can make informed decisions. Encourage critical thinking by asking questions like, "What do you think could happen if someone shared a private photo without permission?" This allows them to reflect on the situation and come to a conclusion rather than just listen to the rules.

Let them know that they can come to you for help.

One of the most effective ways to prevent sexting-related incidents is to create an environment where your child feels safe coming to you if they make a mistake. If they believe they will be punished harshly or shamed, they may try to handle the situation alone, which can often worsen things. Let them know that if they ever feel pressured, make a mistake, or find themselves in a difficult situation, they can come to you without fear of judgment. You can say, "If you ever make a mistake or feel uncomfortable about something online, I want you to know that you can always talk to me. My job is to help you, not to punish you."

It's also important to provide practical steps your child can take if they ever find themself involved in a sexting situation. Teach them that if they receive an inappropriate message or request, they should never respond, screenshot the message for evidence, and report the person to a trusted adult or platform moderators. If they have already sent something, they should stop communicating with the recipient, tell a trusted adult immediately, and take steps to secure their accounts.

Emphasize that self-worth is not tied to online interactions or validation from others.

Many teens engage in sexting because they seek approval or fear rejection. Help them build self-confidence and resilience so they understand that their value is not determined by whether or not they comply with someone else's requests. Remind them that they have the right to say no, the right to protect their privacy, and the right to expect respect in all their interactions.

The conversation about sexting should not be a one-time talk but an ongoing dialogue as your child grows and their online interactions evolve. By maintaining open communication, educating them about the risks, and giving them the tools to make good decisions, you can help them navigate the digital world with confidence and security.

Risks of Pornography Sites

On the internet, pornography is not only accessible but often just a few clicks away, making it a topic that parents cannot afford to overlook. While discussions around this topic traditionally focuses on moral or ethical considerations, it's also crucial to address the significant cybersecurity risks associated with this domain.

Pornography sites are breeding grounds for cyber threats. They are loaded with malware and viruses, with cybercriminals exploiting the high traffic to spread malicious content or collect sensitive data. This can lead to significant emotional and financial distress especially when personal information is at stake. Additionally, phishing scams are rampant, with pop-up ads or fake login pages designed to trick users into divulging personal details that can be used for identity theft or financial fraud.

Cryptojacking is a less visible but equally insidious threat. It involves the unauthorized use of a person's computer to mine cryptocurrency, slowing down the device and increasing energy consumption without the user's knowledge. Malicious actors also use popup redirects, often leading users to fraudulent websites that further compromise security. The sophisticated nature of these attacks underscores the importance of robust cybersecurity practices.

Emerging technologies like deepfakes and AI manipulation add another layer of complexity to the risks associated with pornography sites. Deepfakes involve creating realistic but fake videos or images using artificial intelligence, which can be used to blackmail or deceive individuals. AI manipulation produces convincing but fraudulent content that misleads viewers and spreads misinformation. These technologies have made it more critical than ever for families to remain vigilant and informed about the digital content they consume.

Webcam spying is a particularly invasive threat. Cybercriminals gain unauthorized access to a device's camera and capture images or videos without the user's consent. This invasion of privacy can have serious consequences, including unauthorized personal content distribution. Tracking and data collection are widespread practices on pornography sites, where user behavior is monitored and recorded without consent. This data can be sold to third parties or used to create targeted advertisements, further eroding personal privacy.

Addressing these issues is essential to protecting your family's digital safety and fostering an open and honest relationship regarding online content. Approach the topic of pornography with sensitivity and understanding, recognizing that curiosity is a natural part of growing up. Acknowledge the existence of these sites without judgment. Focus on the potential risks rather than moral implications. Explain that engaging with such content can lead to unintended consequences and long-term privacy breaches.

It's also a good idea to debunk common privacy myths. One such myth is the belief that private browsing, or incognito mode, keeps users safe from threats. While the incognito mode prevents browsing history from being saved on the device, it does not protect against malware, tracking, or data collection. Another misconception is that not clicking on anything will prevent a virus. Unfortunately, visiting a site can sometimes trigger an automatic malware download onto a device.

In summary, while discussing this sensitive topic with your child can feel highly uncomfortable for both parties, understand that fostering open communication and equipping the kids with the knowledge to protect themselves is needed for them to remain safe and make informed choices in the digital age.

Torrent Sites and "Free" Downloads

Many young people use "free" streaming platforms and torrenting sites to download games or movies or listen to music without a cost. But remember: If something is free, then you are the product!

One of the primary dangers associated with torrenting and unauthorized downloads is the presence of malware. Cybercriminals embed malicious software within files that appear to be legitimate games, applications, or media files. Once downloaded, this malware can record keystrokes to steal passwords, encrypt files and demand ransom payments, or grant hackers remote access to a device. In many cases, these infections go undetected until significant damage is done.

Many unofficial download sites and torrent platforms require users to install additional software or create accounts before granting download access. This process involves providing an email address, setting up login credentials, or entering credit card information. These sites may then sell this information to third parties or use it for phishing scams that trick users into revealing even more sensitive details.

Many children and teens are unaware that their innocent attempts to download free content may also carry legal consequences. Copyright laws protect much of the content shared on torrent networks and unofficial download sites, and downloading or distributing such material without authorization is illegal in many countries. In many cases, individuals who engage in piracy have faced fines or legal action from copyright enforcement agencies.

Beyond security risks and legal concerns, unauthorized downloads also severely affect device performance. Many unofficial downloads come bundled with adware or unwanted programs that run in the background, consuming system resources and significantly slowing down a computer or mobile device. Some programs hijack web browsers, replacing search engines with fraudulent versions that track user activity and serve intrusive ads. In extreme cases, a device may become entirely unusable due to the sheer volume of malware installed, leading to costly repairs or a complete system reset.

One of the ways cybercriminals make torrents and unofficial downloads so appealing is by disguising their malicious files as highly sought-after content. For example, a child looking for a newly released video game might come across a torrent claiming to offer a free copy. However, instead of a playable game, the download could contain a trojan that installs spyware or ransomware on the device. In other instances, hackers create fake game modifications, cheats, or premium software cracks, enticing users to install what they believe will enhance their experience.

These threats aren't limited to shady websites. Social media and forums often host fake download links shared by scammers posing as helpful community members. For kids and teens, it's especially hard to tell what's safe and what's not in such cases. Compulsive downloading adds to the risk. Some children develop a habit of constantly seeking new content, making them more likely to ignore warnings or rush installations.

The consequences of unsafe downloading habits extend beyond individual devices. Infected devices connected to a shared home network can spread malware to other devices, putting the entire household at risk. A single compromised laptop or tablet could allow a hacker to access a home's Wi-Fi network, infect other connected devices, and even access sensitive data stored on a family's personal computers. This type of network vulnerability highlights the importance of practicing safe downloading habits and using cybersecurity measures, such as firewalls and up-to-date antivirus software, to protect the entire household.

CHAPTER 11

Digital Well-Being and Algorithmic Addiction

When excessive screen time becomes a security risk

Most conversations around kids and the internet focus on safety, scams, predators, and privacy threats. But even in the absence of danger, a deeper issue persists. Many children today are chronically overstimulated, emotionally hijacked, and mentally exhausted from spending hours on platforms designed not to support them, but to keep them scrolling. It's not always a threat in the traditional sense. But it is a slow, persistent pull away from balance, focus, and self-regulation.

Once children are emotionally dysregulated and locked into constant feedback loops, they become easier targets for cyber threats. Manipulative content, scams, and even predatory groomers rely on catching someone in a moment of vulnerability, which often occurs when the kids are tired, upset, or seeking validation. An overstimulated child scrolling late at night is less likely to question a suspicious link or a message from a stranger.

Algorithmic addiction doesn't just affect mental health, it weakens the very awareness and judgment kids need to stay safe online.

How Algorithms Target Emotional States

Platforms today don't just serve content, they intend to shape moods. Recommendation engines are built to recognize what holds attention, and negative emotions often hold it the longest. A child who lingers slightly longer on a dramatic video, a sad clip, or a comment thread full of outrage will find their feed filled with more of the same.

These systems learn fast. They pick up on behavioral signals, what videos are rewatched, which thumbnails get clicks, and when a child slows their scroll. And when a child is already in an emotionally vulnerable state, angry after a fight, lonely after school, sad without knowing why, the algorithm reinforces the mood. Rage, resentment, and insecurity become good for business.

Dopamine and the attention loop

Dopamine, the brain chemical tied to reward and anticipation, plays a key role in keeping kids locked in. Every Like, every comment, every notification creates a tiny burst. But this stimulation isn't the same as happiness.

And over time, the brain becomes used to the constant reward cycle. Kids may lose patience for slower activities like reading a book or sitting through a class. Without knowing it, they begin to crave the next swipe, the next sound, and the next update. And when nothing's happening on screen, they feel agitated or anxious or irritable without knowing why.

It's a chemical loop designed by experts and tested at scale. And it's important that we stop blaming kids for responding exactly as the system intends.

Choosing Tools That Help

Not all tech is built with the same values. Some apps are designed to keep users passive, endlessly consuming. These platforms bury time spent in vague settings or hide "screen time" data altogether. Others nudge users back in with red badges, autoplay, and infinite scroll.

But there are also tools that promote awareness and self-regulation:

- iOS and Android offer built-in screen time limits and activity reports.
- Apps like Forest encourage focus by growing a tree as kids stay off their phones.
- Browsers like Brave and extensions like uBlock Origin limit distraction-heavy websites.
- Journaling or mindfulness apps like Day One or Headspace give an alternative to scrolling when kids are bored or restless.

Helping your child identify the difference between *tools that use them* and *tools they use* is a powerful step toward digital agency. You don't need to cut off tech to build healthier habits. Small changes, made consistently, are often more effective than rules enforced with resentment.

Some strategies that work in families are:

- **Set device timers** with your child's input, not just your authority.
- **Use greyscale mode** during homework or before bedtime; removing color makes scrolling less appealing.
- **Name the feeling** when they reach for the device: "Are you bored, overwhelmed, or just zoning out?"
- **Take tech-free time together**, not as a punishment, but as a reset.
- **Create a shared family dashboard** for screen time so it feels like teamwork, not surveillance.
- **Encourage one app that creates vs. five that consume**, video editing, music-making, journaling, or storytelling.

It's also okay to say out loud, "These apps are designed to pull us in. It's not your fault." Kids are more likely to listen when they know you're not judging them, but walking alongside them.

Digital well-being isn't about cutting off access. It's about helping kids understand when the tool is useful and when it's using them. By recognizing the emotional pull of algorithms and giving children the language and support to push back, we're not just protecting their focus. We're protecting their sense of self.

And in doing so, we're also protecting them from digital manipulation that often hides in plain sight. When kids develop a sense of control over their screen habits, they're more likely to spot red flags, whether it's a phishing attempt disguised as a giveaway or an online stranger trying to build trust too quickly. Emotional clarity strengthens digital boundaries. The more grounded a child feels in their online habits, the harder it becomes for someone else to hijack their attention, their decisions, or their trust.

However, even with the best awareness, support, and boundaries in place, things can still go wrong. No child is completely immune to the reach of a persistent scammer, a skilled manipulator, or a moment of poor judgment. When that happens, what matters most is how we respond. In the next chapter, let's see how you can best respond when your child is facing an ongoing cyber threat.

Chapter 12

What to Do If Your Child Becomes a Victim

8 Steps to protect, support, and heal

No parent ever wants to imagine their child being targeted online. But even the most careful families might find themselves in that moment, the one where your child comes to you frightened, confused, or ashamed because something has gone wrong.

You've had the talks. You've set the rules. You've done everything you can to keep them safe. But on the day when they come to you, or you notice something's off, your stomach drops. Maybe they got tricked by a scam. Maybe someone pressured them into sharing something private. Maybe they've been carrying this alone for weeks, scared you'll be disappointed. However it happened, and here you are, torn between wanting to fix it *right now* and wishing it had never happened at all.

You're allowed to feel whatever you're feeling, fear, anger, even guilt. But this isn't about what you *should've* done. It's about what your child needs *next*. They don't need lectures on how they should have known better. They just need *you*, calm, steady, and ready to listen before you act.

This chapter is your roadmap for those first raw hours and the days after. We'll cover how to handle the practical stuff (like reporting and damage control) and the harder parts (rebuilding trust, helping the child heal). You don't need to be a cybersecurity expert to do this. You'll just need to be patient, take a few deep breaths, and find the courage to work through what actions to take to protect your child and support their healing.

Let's take this one step at a time.

Step 1: Pause and Breathe

When your child tells you what happened, or when you discover it yourself, your heart might race. You might feel the urge to demand answers, fix it immediately, or even (understandably) let an "I told you so!" slip out. But before you do anything, pause. Take a breath. This moment is fragile.

This isn't about assigning blame. This is about gathering yourself so you can walk forward with your child through what comes next. Because you can't undo what's already happened, but you can respond with clarity, calm, and strength. You can help your child feel safe again. You can show them that mistakes, even serious ones, don't change your care for them and don't mean the story ends there.

Children are susceptible to their parents' emotions, and an overreaction can cause them to feel even more scared, guilty, or reluctant to share information in the future. Keep that in mind and do your best to remain calm.

Your child is watching your reaction more closely than you realize. If they see panic or anger, they may shut down further. If they sense steadiness, they'll feel safer opening up. So, even if your mind is spinning, try to steady your voice and say something like:

"I'm so glad you told me."

"This isn't your fault, and we'll figure it out together."

"You're not in trouble. I am here to help."

If they feel scared, embarrassed, or angry, validate those emotions while reassuring them that the issue can be resolved.

Step 2: Listen Without Interrupting

Your child might hesitate, backtrack, or leave out details at first. That's okay. Don't push. Just listen. The more they feel heard, the more they'll share.

Ask gentle, open-ended questions about the incident:

"Can you tell me what happened?"

"It's OK if you don't remember everything. Just try your best."

"How did this make you feel?"

"Is there anything else you want me to know?"

Resist the urge to say, *"Why did you do that?"* or *"You should have known better."* Right now, they don't need a lecture. They need to know you're on their side.

Step 3: Understand the Threat and What's at Stake

Understanding what happened will help determine the best course of action. As your child narrates the incident, try to gather the important details:

What platform or website did this occur on?

Who was involved? (Was it a stranger, a friend, or someone pretending to be someone they know?)

What was said, shared, or done?

Did they engage with the person or content, and if so, how?

Has this happened before?

If applicable, ask your child to take screenshots or do so yourself before the content disappears. Documentation will be essential if legal action or platform intervention is necessary.

Understanding the threat clearly gives you the power to act wisely, not react out of fear.

Step 4: Assess the Type and Severity of the Threat

Online threats can vary widely in nature and impact. Identify what kind of threat your child has encountered to guide your next steps.

If your child is being harassed, threatened, or embarrassed by others online, whether by strangers or classmates:

- **Block the bully.** Most platforms allow users to block and report harmful individuals.

- **Report to the platform.** Social media sites, forums, and gaming networks have policies against harassment and bullying.

- **Save evidence.** Keep screenshots or logs of the bullying to provide proof if escalation is needed.

- **Monitor your child's emotional well-being.** Encourage open conversations and, if necessary, seek counseling or professional support.

- If an adult or stranger has been attempting to groom, manipulate, or exploit your child:

- **Cease all communication.** Do not respond to the predator.

- **Report to authorities.** In the U.S., the National Center for Missing & Exploited Children (NCMEC) provides resources and reporting tools.

- **Contact law enforcement.** If any illegal activity has taken place, such as requests for explicit photos, immediate intervention is necessary.

- **Strengthen privacy settings.** Ensure your child's online profiles are private and that they are not sharing personal information any further.

- If your child's account has been hacked or their personal information has been compromised:

- **Change all passwords immediately.** Use strong, unique passwords for each platform.

- **Enable two-factor authentication (2FA).** This adds an extra layer of security.
- **Check for unauthorized activity.** Review financial accounts, emails, or messages that may have been accessed.
- **Report to the platform.** Many websites have procedures for recovering hacked accounts.

If your child has been tricked into sending money, sharing sensitive information, or participating in a fraudulent scheme:

- **Contact the payment provider.** If money was sent, you may be able to dispute the transaction.
- **Report to fraud agencies.** See the resources section at the back of this book for the agencies in your country
- **Educate your child about recognizing scams.** Teach them about phishing emails, fake giveaways, and too-good-to-be-true offers.

Step 5: Report the Incident

Depending on the severity of the threat, different reporting measures may be necessary:

- **To the platform:** Websites, social media platforms, and gaming networks often have moderation teams that handle abuse reports.
- **To the school:** Notifying school officials can help resolve the issue if cyberbullying involves classmates.

- **To the police:** If there is evidence of criminal activity, local law enforcement should be contacted.

- **To online safety organizations:** Groups like CyberTipline (NCMEC) or Internet Crimes Against Children (ICAC) Task Forces specialize in handling digital crimes against minors.

Step 6: Provide Emotional Support and Counseling If Needed

Getting hurt online leaves scars you can't see. Your child might be feeling ashamed, scared, or even guilty, like it's their fault. (It's not, ever.) Here's how to be their safe place:

- **Keep communication open.** Let your child know they can always come to you with concerns.

- **Watch for behavioral changes.** Signs of withdrawal, anxiety, or depression may indicate a more profound impact. If necessary, seek professional help. A counselor or therapist specializing in cyber issues can help children process their experiences.

- **Empower them with knowledge.** After the dust settles, teach them safety, not to scare them but to arm them. Knowledge is the best armor.

Step 7: Strengthen Online Safety Measures

Once the immediate threat is addressed, take proactive steps to prevent future risks.

- **Review privacy settings** on all social media accounts and online games.
- **Limit online interactions with strangers.** Teach your child the importance of only engaging with people they know in real life.
- **Educate children about digital literacy.** Teach them to recognize fake accounts, phishing scams, and manipulative tactics predators use.
- **Encourage healthy online habits.** Balance screen time with offline activities and promote critical thinking about online interactions.

Step 8: Watch for Lingering Fear or Shame

After the initial crisis, check-in. Some kids bounce back quickly; others carry the weight longer. Watch for:

- Withdrawal
- Trouble sleeping
- Avoiding devices
- Unusual anger, sadness, or irritability
- Physical complaints with no medical cause

If these behaviors last more than 2-3 weeks or interfere with daily life:

Reassure them with words like *"It's normal to feel upset after what happened. We'll get through this together."*

Adjust their routine to temporarily reduce screen time if it causes stress.

Get professional help from a child psychologist or school counselor who can provide trauma support.

While encountering online threats can be frightening, they can also be an opportunity for growth and education. Proper steps can resolve the immediate issue and help your child develop more potent digital literacy and resilience.

Your involvement in their online life, through guidance, open conversations, and proactive safety measures, will be key in helping them navigate the internet safely and responsibly.

CHAPTER 13

Tools and Resources

Must-have resources for ongoing cyber protection

The internet is constantly evolving, and so are the threats that come with it. As new scams and social engineering techniques emerge, staying safe online requires more than just a one-time lesson. Cybersecurity is not a set-it-and-forget-it practice but a continuing process requiring vigilance, learning, and adaptation. Fortunately, various tools, programs, and educational resources are designed to help families stay ahead of cyber threats and thrive in a secure digital environment.

From password managers and parental control software to reputable cybersecurity websites and online safety courses, having the right tools can make all the difference in preventing cyberattacks, protecting personal data, and ensuring that children develop strong, lifelong digital safety habits. Teaching kids how to recognize and use these tools empowers them to take an active role in cybersecurity rather than relying solely on parents or schools to protect them.

This chapter will explore the most effective cybersecurity tools available today. It will also highlight trusted organizations and websites that provide up-to-date information on cyber threats and best practices.

Real-Time Network Monitoring

Many parents focus on monitoring their child's devices, but what about the network?

This is where real-time network monitoring comes in. Network monitoring helps you keep track of all the devices that connect to your home Wi-Fi and alerts you if anything unusual happens. With the right tools, you can see which devices are online, detect suspicious activity, block unsafe connections, and protect your household from cyber threats.

For example, your child could accidentally connect to a risky website, or a hacker could try to sneak into your home Wi-Fi network. With real-time monitoring, you can spot these issues instantly and take action before they become serious problems.

Network monitoring also ensures that your child is using the internet safely. Many parents worry about what their kids are consuming online, and network monitoring provides a bird's-eye view of all online activity without being intrusive. Instead of checking your child's device manually, a network monitoring tool allows you to set up automatic alerts and block dangerous activity before it happens.

Some network monitoring tools also let you set time limits on devices, making it easier to enforce healthy digital habits. You can also block access to certain websites to ensure your child isn't exposed to harmful material.

Parents can install several easy-to-use tools to monitor and secure their home network. Some are built into Wi-Fi routers, while others require separate apps or devices. Following are some of the best options.

Router-based monitoring

Many modern Wi-Fi routers have built-in network security features. If your router doesn't have built-in monitoring features, you can upgrade to a smart router with better security options. Many of these routers allow you to receive instant alerts if an unknown device connects to your network or your child visits a blocked website.

Network security apps

If you don't want to replace your router, use network security apps that work alongside your existing Wi-Fi setup. These apps help monitor all connected devices and provide alerts for suspicious activity. Some options are

OpenDNS (Cisco Umbrella): A cloud-based security tool that automatically blocks access to malicious websites and allows parents to filter content based on age-appropriateness.

Find: A popular home network monitoring app that helps you see all devices connected to your Wi-Fi and detect intruders.

Circle with Disney: A device that connects to your Wi-Fi and gives you complete control over internet activity, including setting time limits and monitoring browsing history.

Parental Control Tools

Parental control tools help parents manage how their children use the Internet. They come in different forms: some are built into devices, some are apps that can be installed, and others are network-based tools that protect every device connected to the home Wi-Fi.

These tools allow parents to:

- **Filter inappropriate content** so kids don't accidentally stumble upon adult material, violence, or harmful sites.
- **Limit screen time** to prevent excessive gaming or social media use.
- **Monitor social media and chat activity** to protect against online predators and cyberbullying.
- **Block specific apps or websites** that might be risky or distracting.
- **Set internet curfews** so devices automatically disconnect from Wi-Fi at bedtime or during homework hours.

These protections can be customized based on a child's age and maturity level, giving them the right amount of freedom while keeping them safe.

Some parents worry that setting up parental controls means they are spying on their kids. But the goal is not to invade their privacy, it's to create a safe online space where they can learn and grow while avoiding digital dangers.

Many parental control options are available, so choosing the right one depends on how much monitoring you need and what works best for your family.

Built-in parental controls on devices

Most smartphones, tablets, gaming consoles, and computers have built-in free parental control settings. These settings allow users to block content, set time limits, and restrict in-app purchases. Some commonly used options are:

- *Apple Screen Time for iPhones, iPads, and MacBooks*
- *Google Family Link for Android devices*
- *Windows and Xbox Family Settings*

These built-in controls are great because they are free and easy to use, but they work best for younger children who mostly use one or two devices.

Apps for more advanced monitoring

If your child uses multiple devices or you want more detailed control, certain parental control apps provide a more complete way to manage online activity.

- **Bark** is one of the best tools for monitoring social media, text messages, and emails. It uses AI to detect potential dangers such as cyberbullying, online predators, and self-harm language and alert parents if something concerning occurs.

- **Qustodio** provides real-time screen time tracking, content filtering, and location tracking, making it great for parents who want a mix of monitoring and digital wellness features.
- **Net Nanny** offers strong website blocking and content filtering, preventing children from accessing harmful sites while allowing them to use the internet safely.

These apps work across multiple devices, making them ideal for parents who need to manage internet use across phones, tablets, and computers.

Parental control tool selection checklist

Use this checklist to help you choose the right parental control tool for your family:

- Evaluate the features: Are customizable screen time limits and content filters available?
- Check compatibility: Does the tool work with all your family's devices?
- Assess ease of use: Is the interface intuitive for quick adjustments?
- Consider budget: Does the cost align with your financial plans?
- Look for additional features: Are real-time monitoring and location tracking included?

While parental control tools are powerful, they work best with open conversations about online safety. Here's how to set them up so kids can develop good digital habits without feeling like they're constantly being watched.

First, explain why you're using parental controls. Instead of saying, *"I don't trust you,"* frame it as: *"I want to ensure you have a safe and positive experience online."* This helps children understand that these tools are meant to protect, not punish.

Next, choose the right level of control based on your child's age. Younger kids may need more restrictions, like strict content filtering and app approvals, while teenagers may only need screen time limits and social media monitoring. Adjust settings as your child grows and shows responsibility.

Review the settings regularly. The internet changes constantly, and children's needs evolve. Check-in every few months to update restrictions, adjust screen time settings, and discuss any concerns your child may have.

Finally, don't rely solely on parental controls. While these tools are excellent for blocking harmful content and managing screen time, they are not a substitute for teaching children how to navigate the internet responsibly. Talk to them about online privacy, recognizing scams, and knowing when to ask for help.

Balancing Safety with Privacy

Some children may feel that monitoring tools or parental controls invade their privacy, especially as they age. Finding the right balance between protecting them from harm and giving them the freedom to grow is essential.

Instead of secretly tracking everything your child does, use parental controls to guide them toward responsible internet use. Let them know what's being monitored and why. Feeling included in the process makes them more likely to independently make smart, safe choices.

For older kids, gradually easing restrictions can help build trust. Instead of blocking everything outright, start with content warnings and time limits, then adjust based on their behavior and maturity level.

Staying Informed with Trusted Cybersecurity Information

Next comes staying informed about cybersecurity. As parents, you face the challenge of keeping up with the latest digital threats that your children may encounter. Understanding the changing landscape allows you to anticipate potential risks and vulnerabilities, equipping you to protect your family more effectively.

Government and law enforcement websites

One of the best ways to get accurate, up-to-date cybersecurity advice is through official government and law enforcement websites. These sources provide free, reliable information, from online scams to protecting your child's privacy.

See the resources section at the back of this book for the appropriate contacts for your country.

Cybersecurity blogs and news sites

For parents who want regular updates on new threats, cybersecurity blogs and news websites are a great way to stay informed. These sites explain complex cybersecurity topics in simple language so that non-technical users can understand the risks and how to avoid them. Here are a few examples to get you started.

Cybersecurity Coach

Cybersecurity Coach provides helpful tips and tricks, and you can receive the latest news on hacks and breaches in your inbox. Website: www.CybersecurityCoachOnline.com

The CyberWire

A daily cybersecurity news site that provides brief, easy-to-understand updates on the latest threats, making it perfect for busy parents who want a quick way to stay informed. Website: www.thecyberwire.com

These sites translate technical topics into everyday language, making them useful for non-tech-savvy parents who want clear, actionable advice.

Some parents prefer to listen to experts speak rather than read long articles. YouTube and podcasts are great ways to learn about online safety in a simple, engaging format.

The *Ask Leo!* YouTube Channel

Run by tech expert Leo Notenboom, this channel covers internet safety basics for non-technical users, including how to spot scams, avoid phishing, and secure family devices. Channel: www.youtube.com/@askleonotenboom

Smashing Security Podcast

This lighthearted but informative podcast covers the latest cyber threats in a way that's easy to understand. It's an excellent way for parents to stay informed without feeling overwhelmed. Website: www.smashingsecurity.com

The CyberWire Daily Podcast

A short, daily update on cybersecurity news, perfect for parents who want a quick, digestible way to keep up with online threats. Website: www.thecyberwire.com/podcasts/daily-podcast

Social media communities and forums for parents

Sometimes, the best advice comes from other parents dealing with the same concerns. Social media groups and forums allow parents to ask questions, share experiences, and learn from one another.

r/Parenting on Reddit

A large parenting community (found at www.reddit.com/r/Parenting) where people share advice on keeping kids safe online and managing screen time.

Facebook Groups

Many Facebook groups (search "Online safety for parents") focus on cybersecurity and parenting, offering tips, discussions, and real-world experiences from other parents.

Common Sense Media Parent Discussion Boards

A trusted platform (found at www.commonsensemedia.org) where parents can talk about internet safety, gaming risks, and social media concerns.

These groups provide real-world advice from parents learning to keep their children safe online. The internet is constantly changing, but we as parents can protect our children from cyber risks with the correct information and right guidance. The key is to stay curious, ask questions, and use reliable resources.

Chapter 14

Interactive Activities

Engaging Kids in Cyber Safety

Simply telling kids about online dangers may not always be enough. Many children learn best through interactive activities that engage them in fun and meaningful ways.

Children are more likely to remember and apply lessons when they are actively involved in the learning process. Instead of relying on lectures or strict rules, parents can use games, role-playing, challenges, and real-world scenarios to help kids understand the importance of cybersecurity.

Here are some practical and fun activities parents can use to make cyber safety lessons more engaging.

The Password Strength Challenge

Instead of just telling kids to use strong passwords, make it a fun challenge!

Activity: "Can You Hack It?"

Write down 5–10 weak passwords on separate pieces of paper (examples: "123456," "password," "mypetdog," or "iloveyou").

Lay them out face-up. Set a timer for one minute and ask your child: "You're the hacker now, which password would you try first, and why?"

Let them pick passwords they think would be easiest to guess, and have them explain their reasoning.

Discuss why short, simple passwords are dangerous and how hackers use guessing tools to crack them.

Have them create a super-strong password using three or more random words (for example: "BlueBananaRocket47!").

Finally, test their password together using an online strength checker like . Celebrate if it's strong, and if it's not, work together to improve it!

The Cyber Scavenger Hunt

This activity helps kids spot privacy risks in their digital world.

Activity: "Find the Hidden Clues"

Ask your child to check their social media profiles, gaming accounts, or online profiles (with your supervision).

Give them a checklist of private information to search for, including:

- Full name
- Age or birthday
- School name
- Home address or location

- Photos with personal details (such as a school logo on a hoodie)

Each time they find a piece of private information, discuss why it could be risky and how to adjust privacy settings to hide it.

The Cyberbullying Role-Play

Cyberbullying is a significant issue for kids and teens. Instead of just warning kids about it, help them experience how different online interactions feel through role-playing.

Activity: "What Would You Do?"

Create a scenario where one person sends a mean or inappropriate message online.

Have your child role-play as the victim and talk about how it would make them feel.

Switch roles and have them pretend to be a bystander who witnesses cyberbullying.

Discuss what they could do in real life, such as:

- Blocking or reporting the bully
- Talking to a trusted adult
- Supporting the victim instead of staying silent

Safe Search Challenge

Not all websites are safe; some search results can lead to inappropriate or harmful content. This game helps kids practice using safe search tools.

Activity: "Find the Right Answer"

Give your child a safe topic to research online (for example: "How do airplanes fly?").

Ask them to find three good websites with safe and accurate information.

Teach them how to spot untrustworthy websites, such as:

- Sites with lots of pop-up ads
- Fake news sites with extreme claims
- Websites without HTTPS (secure connection)

Show them how to use safe search tools, such as Google SafeSearch.

Family Cyber Contract

Creating a family agreement about online rules is a fun and straightforward way to get kids involved in cyber safety.

Activity: "Write Your Own Rules"

Sit down as a family and list the most important online safety rules (examples: No sharing passwords, no talking to strangers, screen time limits).

Let your child contribute their ideas to make it fair and balanced.

Write down the rules, sign them together, and display them somewhere visible (like on the fridge).

Final Thoughts

As we approach the end of our journey, I want to reflect on what we've covered. Throughout this book, we've explored the myriad challenges families face in the digital age, from understanding the evolving threats to developing practical strategies for protecting our loved ones online. We've discussed the complexities of social media, examined the risks of online gaming, and navigated the sensitive topics that often arise in the context of digital safety.

At the heart of this book lies a fundamental truth: cybersecurity awareness is not just a luxury but a necessity in today's world. However, knowledge alone is not enough. Open communication between parents and children is the cornerstone of adequate digital safety.

By fostering an environment of trust and dialogue, we create a space where our kids feel comfortable sharing their online experiences, both positive and negative. This open exchange allows us to guide them through their challenges, offering support and wisdom. Remember, our children look to us as role models. By demonstrating positive digital citizenship, we set the stage for them to follow.

Of course, the journey towards comprehensive online safety is ongoing. The strategies and tools discussed in this book provide a solid foundation, but it's up to you to take proactive steps to implement them in your daily life. Whether you set up parental controls, create strong passwords, or regularly review privacy settings, each action contributes to a more secure environment for your loved ones. Small changes can significantly impact your safety, and every effort counts.

And don't stop there. Continue to educate yourself about the latest trends and developments in cybersecurity. Use online resources, attend community workshops, and participate in discussions that keep you informed and empowered. You'll be better equipped to navigate the internet and protect your family from emerging threats by staying vigilant and adaptable.

As we conclude this book, I am grateful for your commitment to your family's online safety. By reading this book and engaging with its content, you've already taken a significant step toward creating a more secure digital future for your loved ones. Remember, you're not alone in this journey. Countless families like yours are working together to promote digital safety and build a better online world for future generations.

So, take the lessons you've learned and apply them confidently. Share your experiences and insights with others, and don't hesitate to seek support when needed. Together, we can create a digital environment that fosters growth, connection, and security for all.

As you embark on this next chapter, I leave you with this final thought: you can make a difference. Every choice you make, every conversation you have, and every action you take contributes to the collective well-being of our online community. Embrace this responsibility with courage and determination, knowing your efforts will help shape a brighter, safer future for your family and beyond.

Thank you for joining me on this journey. I wish you all the best as you continue to navigate the complex yet rewarding world of online safety.

Remember, you're not alone, you've got this!

Glossary

2FA (Two-Factor Authentication)

A security method that requires two forms of identification to access an account. Typically, this means something you know (like a password) and something you have (like a code sent to your phone or an app). 2FA makes it much harder for hackers to break into your accounts, even if they steal your password.

Adware

Software that automatically displays or downloads advertising material when a user is online, often without clearly asking for permission.

Antivirus Software

A program designed to detect and remove malicious software (malware), including viruses, from your computer or device.

App (Application)

A piece of software that runs on a computer, phone, or tablet. Apps can be useful or harmful, depending on how they're designed and used.

Authentication

The process of verifying who someone is. Usually done through passwords, but can also involve fingerprints, facial recognition, or security codes.

Backup

A copy of important files or data saved in another location (like the cloud or an external hard drive) in case the original is lost or damaged.

Breach (Data Breach)

When private or confidential information is accessed or stolen by someone without permission, often from companies or websites.

Browser

The software used to access the internet (e.g., Chrome, Safari, Firefox). Keeping your browser up to date is important for security.

Catfishing

Pretending to be someone else online, usually to scam or manipulate others, especially on social media or dating platforms.

Clickjacking

A trick where a user clicks on something they think is safe, but it secretly does something harmful, like sharing information or downloading malware.

Cloud Storage

Saving files on the internet (like Google Drive, iCloud, or Dropbox) instead of just on your device. It's convenient but should be secured with strong passwords.

Cyberbullying

Using digital devices, apps, or websites to harass, threaten, or embarrass someone, often repeatedly.

Cybercrime

Any crime that involves a computer, network, or digital device. Includes hacking, identity theft, online scams, and more.

Cybersecurity

The practice of protecting computers, networks, and personal information from digital attacks and unauthorized access.

Dark Web

A part of the internet that isn't indexed by search engines and is often used for illegal activity. It's not the same as the 'deep web.'

Deepfake

A digitally manipulated video or audio clip that makes it look or sound like someone said or did something they didn't. Often used to spread misinformation.

Digital Footprint

The trail of data you leave behind when you use the internet, like social media posts, website visits, or online purchases.

Doxxing

Publishing someone's private or personal information online, usually to shame or harm them.

Encryption

The process of converting information into a code to protect it from unauthorized access.

Firewall

A security system that controls what data can come in and out of your network, blocking suspicious activity.

Grooming (Online Grooming)

When an adult builds a relationship with a child or teen online to exploit or abuse them, often through flattery or manipulation.

Hack/Hacking

Gaining unauthorized access to a computer or online account. Not all hackers are bad, but many do it for harmful reasons.

Identity Theft

When someone steals your personal information (like your Social Security number or credit card details) and pretends to be you.

MFA (Multi-Factor Authentication)

An extra layer of security that requires more than just a password, like a code sent to your phone or a fingerprint scan.

Malware

Malicious software designed to harm or exploit devices, networks, or users. Types include viruses, worms, spyware, and ransomware.

Online Predator

Someone who uses the internet to exploit vulnerable people, especially children or teens, often for sexual or financial reasons.

Parental Controls

Tools and settings that let you limit or monitor your child's online activity, on phones, games, websites, and streaming services.

Password Manager

A secure app or software that stores all your passwords so you don't have to remember them. It can also help you create strong ones.

Phishing

A scam where someone tries to trick you into giving away personal info (like passwords or credit card numbers) by pretending to be a trusted source.

Privacy Settings

Options on apps and websites that control who can see your information or contact you.

Ransomware

Malware that locks you out of your computer or files until you pay a ransom to get access back.

Scam

A dishonest attempt to trick you out of money or personal information. Online scams can happen through email, social media, texts, and fake websites.

Screen Time

The amount of time spent on digital devices. Managing screen time is important for mental, emotional, and physical health.

Social Engineering

Tricking people into giving up private information (like passwords) by pretending to be someone trustworthy.

Spam

Unwanted or junk messages, usually promotional or fraudulent, often sent in bulk.

Spyware

Malware that secretly watches what you do on your device, tracking keystrokes, browsing history, or personal info.

Terms of Service

The rules you agree to when you use a website, app, or game. It's where you'll find info about privacy, data use, and what they can or can't do with your info.

Tracking Cookies

Small pieces of data stored on your device by websites to track your activity online, often for advertising purposes.

Trojan Horse (Trojan)

A type of malware that looks like a normal file or app but secretly does something harmful once installed.

Two-Step Verification

Another name for Multi-Factor Authentication. It means you need two ways to prove your identity to log in, like a password and a code sent to your phone.

URL (Uniform Resource Locator)

The web address of a site or page (like www.example.com). Always check that URLs are correct to avoid phishing sites.

Update (Software Update)

New versions of software or apps that fix bugs and improve security. Keeping your apps updated helps protect your devices.

VPN (Virtual Private Network)

A service that hides your online activity and location by sending your internet traffic through a secure connection.

Virus

A type of malware that spreads from one device to another, often deleting files or damaging systems.

Wi-Fi

Wireless internet connection. Make sure your home Wi-Fi is secured with a strong password.

Zero-Day

A security flaw that hackers discover before the company knows about it or fixes it. These are very dangerous because they're unknown and unpatched.

References

Federal Bureau of Investigation. (2023). Online Child Exploitation Statistics. Retrieved from https://www.fbi.gov

National Center for Missing and Exploited Children. (2023). Online Enticement of Children Report. Retrieved from https://www.missingkids.org

Homeland Security Investigations. (2023). Sextortion Case Reports. Retrieved from https://www.ice.gov/features/sextortion

CNN. (2017, July). Teen's death linked to Blue Whale Challenge raises alarm. Retrieved from https://www.cnn.com

Wired. (2024). Lancaster Country Day School students charged in deepfake image scandal. Retrieved from https://www.wired.com

The Guardian. (2017). Kansas man killed in 'swatting' incident after online feud. Retrieved from https://www.theguardian.com

YouTube Help. (2024). Understanding Elsagate and the crackdown on child-endangering content. Retrieved from https://support.google.com/youtube

TikTok. (2024). Safety and Privacy Resources for Families. Retrieved from https://www.tiktok.com/safety

Instagram Help Center. (2024). Family Safety Tools and Privacy Controls. Retrieved from https://help.instagram.com

Snapchat Safety Center. (2024). Keeping Teens Safe on Snapchat. Retrieved from https://www.snapchat.com/safety

Federal Trade Commission. (2024). Scams, Phishing, and Fraud Education for Families. Retrieved from https://www.consumer.ftc.gov

Internet Crime Complaint Center (IC3). (2024). Report Internet Crimes Involving Minors. Retrieved from https://www.ic3.gov

Pew Research Center. (2023). Teens, Social Media, and Technology Use. Retrieved from https://www.pewresearch.org

Common Sense Media. (2023). The State of Kids and Media Use. Retrieved from https://www.commonsensemedia.org

Norton LifeLock. (2024). Top 10 Cybersecurity Threats for Kids in 2024. Retrieved from https://us.norton.com/blog

Alex East. (2023). Cybersecurity for Seniors Made Easy. Magrathea Ventures Inc.

Resources: Help, Reporting & Support

If you or your child encounters a serious online threat, don't wait. Use the resources below to get support, report the incident, or educate yourself further.

United States

National Center for Missing and Exploited Children (NCMEC)

Website: https://www.missingkids.org

Report Child Exploitation: https://report.cybertip.org

Phone: 1-800-THE-LOST (1-800-843-5678)

24/7 hotline for reporting suspected child exploitation.

CyberTipline (Operated by NCMEC)

Online Reporting: https://report.cybertip.org

For reporting online enticement, child sexual abuse material, or inappropriate contact.

Federal Bureau of Investigation (FBI) – Internet Crime Complaint Center (IC3)

Website: https://www.ic3.gov

For reporting internet fraud, hacking, sextortion, and other crimes.

StopBullying.gov

Website: https://www.stopbullying.gov

Resources on preventing and addressing cyberbullying.

Common Sense Media

Website: https://www.commonsensemedia.org

Guides for parents about age-appropriate apps, games, and digital well-being.

U.S. Department of Justice – Sextortion Help

Website: https://www.justice.gov/sextortion

Canada

Cybertip.ca (Operated by the Canadian Centre for Child Protection)

Website: https://www.cybertip.ca

Report child exploitation, sextortion, or suspicious contact.

Phone (Toll-Free): 1-866-658-9022

Canadian Centre for Child Protection (C3P)

Website: https://www.protectchildren.ca

Educational tools and resources for parents, educators, and youth.

RCMP National Child Exploitation Coordination Centre

Website: https://www.rcmp-grc.gc.ca/en/national-child-exploitation-coordination-centre

NeedHelpNow.ca

Website: https://www.needhelpnow.ca

Guidance for teens and parents on dealing with the sharing of sexual images and videos.

MediaSmarts

Website: https://mediasmarts.ca

Digital literacy education for families and schools.

United Kingdom

CEOP (Child Exploitation and Online Protection Command)

Report Abuse: https://www.ceop.police.uk/Safety-Centre

Part of the UK National Crime Agency – for reporting sexual exploitation or grooming.

NSPCC (National Society for the Prevention of Cruelty to Children)

Website: https://www.nspcc.org.uk

Helpline: 0808 800 5000 (for adults)

Childline: 0800 1111 (for children and teens)Email: help@nspcc.org.uk

Internet Watch Foundation (IWF)

Website: https://www.iwf.org.uk

To report child sexual abuse imagery or content.

Thinkuknow (run by CEOP/NCA)

Website: https://www.thinkuknow.co.uk

Age-appropriate safety education for children and parents.

Childnet International

Website: https://www.childnet.com

Advice and toolkits for families on online safety.

Stay One Step Ahead of Scammers!

If you're ready to take control of your digital security, it's important to stay up-to-date with the latest information. Here's what you get when you sign up:

- Tips and tricks to stay safe from online scammers.
- The latest news on breaches that may include your personal information.
- Stories shared by people like you and me.
- Special offers to that can help you secure yourself and your loved ones.
- Much, much more

Made in the USA
Monee, IL
04 November 2026

67404523R00115